Clint Bonner

A HYMN IS BORN

Wilcox and Follett Company

CHICAGO   *New York*   *Toronto*

Manufactured in the United States of America.
Published Simultaneously in Canada by Ambassador Books, Limited.

FIRST PRINTING
1st Printing

Dedication

To two noble souls who first taught me to love the hymns of the church — my
Mother and my Father — the latter being

A PREACHER I KNOW

There are men who toil to build a name;
  Who squander life for wealth and fame,
I know a man who counts no gold;
  Whose treasure is a brother's soul.

For three score years and more than ten
  He's lived his life for other men;
In modest church and humble home
  With scarce a day to call his own.

No choir in robes behind him sings;
  No chime in roof above him rings;
He quotes no lines that men prepare
  But from his heart he reads a prayer.

The hymns he sings are those I know;
  The ones he taught me years ago,
"On Jordan's Stormy Banks I Stand"
  And "Hold to God's Unchanging Hand."

Beside the tomb when teardrops start
  He gently mends a broken heart;
And children gather 'round his knee
  To hear him tell of Galilee.

A thousand souls are waiting there,
  The day he comes their joy to share;
A thousand souls he showed the way
  To life and love and endless day.

                              CLINT BONNER

Preface

Few hymns of the church have been written on assignment. With rare exceptions the stately old hymns that have stood the test of time are the result of experiences that inspired the authors to write them. Even in the exceptional cases the authors found the necessity of (as Fanny Crosby put it) "creating a mood" or inspiration before attempting to write their verse. Thus, there is a story — a human interest story — behind the writing of practically all the time-honored church hymns. And, by knowing the story, there is created a greater appreciation and interest in the hymn. Therein lies the purpose of this collection — to foster a renewed appreciation for the inspiring hymns of our churches.

To gather material upon which these stories are based, obviously, has necessitated diversified research. There are many excellent books for the student of hymnology. These have been drawn upon for pertinent data. Histories, biographical works, and encyclopedias have been extensively used. In addition, the author is indebted to relatives and friends of some of the more recent hymn writers as well as to newspaper editors who have been most helpful in gathering material in their respective localities.

I make no claim to being an authority on theology, hymnology, or the merits of hymns as literature. I willingly leave these subjects to those more qualified. While it is hoped that the material herein contained may be of value to the student, these stories were not written for that purpose.

This book is, in the main, a collection of stories that have appeared once each week (and are appearing at the time of this writing) in newspapers from coast to coast. Therefore, the material has had the advantage of being subjected to criticism of readers that are counted in the millions. All expressions of criticism have been carefully examined and given consideration before compiling the collection into this permanent form.

In the selection of subjects I have tried to represent a wide variety of denominations. No partiality is intended should one denomination be represented more than another. The reader should bear in mind that this is a limited collection and, also, that stories of many noble hymns have not yet come to light.

I have included a number of "gospel songs" which exacting critics do not place in the category of the more stately "hymn." Here again comes to surface the thinking of the newspaper man. I have written for the layman — the man of the masses — and have made no attempt to draw a line between the works of Fanny Crosby, Philip Bliss, and Will Thompson and those of scholarly Charles Wesley, Isaac Watts, and William Cowper. To me, each of the authors represented in this book had one common purpose in mind — to make his or her contribution to Christian worship. And, to me, not one of them has done a job lacking of admiration. And so, to me, all Christian songs are "hymns."

The hymns in this collection are presented in the versions which, in my judgment, are in the most popular use. Many of the older hymns have been altered to varying degrees by editors of hymnals. As originally written, some hymns consisted of a dozen or more verses, from which editors have made varying selections, not only of verses but of lines from verses, in preparing their books. I myself have attempted no such alterations, nor have I adhered to the original except where the original was in popular use. My role has simply been to select widely-used versions as they appear in current hymnals.

It is hoped that these stories will serve the purpose for which they were written — to encourage appreciation for the inspiring hymns of the church which, on their individual merits, they so rightly deserve.

Birmingham, Alabama, 1952   *Clint Bonner*

Acknowledgments

The author is deeply grateful to Mr. John D. Raridan, executive editor of The Brush-Moore Newspapers, Canton, Ohio, for aid in research on Mr. Will Thompson; to Mr. Kendall White of the Elgin, Ill., *Daily Courier-News* for aid in compiling data on Dion De Marbelle; to Dr. Haldor Lillenas for permission to reprint Charles Fillmore's "Tell Mother I'll Be There"; and to Messrs. Gordon and Herbert Shorney of the Hope Publishing Co., Chicago, for invaluable aid in research and for permission to reprint a selection of numbers under their copyright.

Acknowledgments

Table of Contents

A Hymn Is Born

A Rebellious Youth Revolutionizes Church Singing

The clerk read a Psalm and everybody sang. That is, everybody sang except young Isaac Watts. After church that Sunday in 1692 when his Puritan father called him on the carpet, Isaac said flatly that there was no music in the Psalms — and that was that. Whereupon the outraged deacon suggested that the young upstart write something better. The result of that sarcastic challenge was a revolution in church singing that has resounded for two and a half centuries.

Staid old Enoch Watts must not have been thinking when he hurled that dare at his ugly little teen-age son. For at his boarding school in Southampton the deacon himself had taught Isaac five languages before the boy was fourteen. At least, the deacon taught when he wasn't in jail for acts against the Established Church. And for twelve years Mrs. Watts had tutored her oldest son in the writing of verse. At seven he had won a copper medal for writing rhymes. He waxed so poetical in fact that when Enoch threatened to thrash him for rhyming even his everyday conversation, the boy cried out, "O father do some pity take, and I will no more verses make!"

Accepting his father's challenge, 18-year-old Isaac Watts set about "Christianizing and modernizing" the Psalms. It had been tried before, but not by a mind like that of Watts.

The following Sunday the clerk read a new kind of hymn. It began: "Behold the glories of the Lamb amidst His Father's throne; prepare new honors for His name, and songs before unknown." The congregation went wild. They made young Watts bring in one of his "modernized" Psalms every Sunday for two years!

Isaac Watts had successfully broken a tradition. Before he was thirty he wrote "Joy to the World," "When I Can Read My Title Clear," "Am I a Soldier of the Cross?" and 650 other notable hymns, and paved the way for Wesley, Newton, Cowper, and many another. And thus, with Isaac Watts' bold departure from Psalm singing, Christianity found a new medium of worship.

Isaac Watts lived in troubled times, but he could have written no more appropriately for the present era than when he paraphrased the 90th Psalm and wrote:

O GOD, OUR HELP IN AGES PAST

By Isaac Watts, 1674–1748

O God, our help in ages past,
Our hope for years to come,
Our shelter from the stormy blast,
And our eternal home!

Under the shadow of Thy throne,
Still may we dwell secure;
Sufficient in Thine arm alone,
And our defense is sure.

Before the hills in order stood,
Or earth received her frame,
From everlasting Thou art God,
To endless years the same.

O God, our help in ages past,
Our hope for years to come;
Be Thou our guide while life shall last,
And our eternal home.

A Preacher's Visit Lasts
Thirty-six Years

The Lord Mayor was there. Like other elite members of London's great Mark Lane Church, His Honor rarely missed a sermon by the renowned Dr. Watts.

Isaac Watts was young for the pulpit at Mark Lane. Thirty-eight he was now, but he had been at the big church ever since he was twenty-six. He was small — just five feet — and his big head made his small body look even smaller and his long hook nose made his homely face even uglier. He was sickly, too. Hardly had he seen a well day since smallpox nearly killed him when he was fifteen. At Mark Lane he rarely preached two Sundays in succession, but the congregation wouldn't let him quit. They hired an assistant and told Dr. Watts to preach when he felt like it.

A few years after he had his "great and dangerous illness" the ugly little dwarf was sought out by a beautiful lady who had fallen in love with him through his poetry. Her name was Elizabeth Singer; and when Watts saw her he fell head over heels in love. He proposed marriage, but Miss Singer shied away with the remark that she "admired the jewel but could never love the casket." Abandoning hope of marriage the little man wrote, "How vain are all things here below; how false and yet how fair."

Isaac Watts preached that Sunday in 1712, but he didn't feel like it. So the Lord Mayor and Lady Abney carried him out to their mansion in the country. A week's rest, they said, would do him good.

At the Abney home Watts fell in love again — with the three little daughters of his hosts. He wrote verses for them about the "busy little bee" and dogs that "delight to bark and bite," and he wrote a cradle song that began "Hush, my dear, lie still and slumber; holy angels guard thy bed."

The Abneys became so attached to their guest that they wouldn't allow him to leave. In 1720 Watts collected his juvenile verse into his classic *Divine and Moral Songs for Children*. The book sold 80,000

4

copies a year and six generations were raised on it. Watts died, still a bachelor, at the Abney home in 1748 — thirty-six years after going there for a week's rest.

Perhaps Isaac Watts was thinking of his pockmarked face and dwarfed body when, while with the Abneys, he wrote one of the finest hymns ever written:

ALAS! AND DID MY SAVIOUR BLEED?

By Isaac Watts, 1674–1748

Alas, and did my Saviour bleed?
And did my Sovereign die?
Would He devote that sacred head,
For such a worm as I?

Was it for crimes that I have done
He groaned upon the tree?
Amazing pity! grace unknown!
And love beyond degree!

Well might the sun in darkness hide,
And shut his glories in,
When Christ, the mighty Maker, died
For man, the creature's sin.

But drops of grief can ne'er repay
The debt of love I owe;
Here, Lord, I give myself away,
'Tis all that I can do.

5

"*The Greatest Hymn in the English Language*"

To attempt to single out any one hymn as "the greatest ever written" would create as much controversy as adjudging any one United States president as the "greatest in American history." Research on hymnody reveals many marked differences in opinions. But, in the final analysis, public acceptance over a long period seems to be the safest yardstick by which to measure the quality of hymns. This being the case, then, there are many grand hymns that could be called "greatest," but to select any one of the group would be simply a matter of personal preference.

Some years ago in England 3,500 citizens were asked to list, in order, their one hundred favorite hymns. August Toplady's "Rock of Ages" led 3,213 of the lists. Yet, Alfred Lord Tennyson, who certainly knew his poetry and hymns, regarded Reginald Heber's "Holy, Holy, Holy" as the finest of them all.

Because few of the great poets have written hymns, some critics are reluctant even to regard hymn writers as poets. Yet, after listing hymns by Bryant, Whittier, Holmes, and Longfellow, one critic opined that Joseph Gilmore's "My Faith Looks Up To Thee" was superior to them all — and Gilmore did not even claim to be a poet!

Critic Samuel Johnson rather charitably and reluctantly mentioned Isaac Watts in his "Lives of the Poets," but apologized by saying that the little bachelor had only done "better what no man has done well." But another noted critic, Matthew Arnold, so admired the poetry of Watts that he sang and quoted "When I Survey the Wondrous Cross" until ten minutes before he died. And so go the opinions.

In their various ways there were many "greatest" presidents and, because they have stood the test of time, there are many "greatest" hymns. The one Matthew Arnold called "the greatest in the English language" was written in 1707 and is still sung around the world:

When I Survey the Wondrous Cross

By Isaac Watts, 1674–1748

When I survey the wondrous cross,
On which the Prince of glory died,
My richest gain I count but loss,
And pour contempt on all my pride.

Forbid it, Lord! that I should boast,
Save in the death of Christ my God;
All the vain things that charm me most,
I sacrifice them to His blood.

See, from His head, His hands, His feet,
Sorrow and love flow mingled down;
Did e'er such love and sorrow meet,
Or thorns compose so rich a crown?

Were the whole realm of nature mine,
That were a present far too small;
Love so amazing, so divine,
Demands my soul, my life, my all.

Neither Poet nor Composer Knew He Was Writing a Christmas Carol

Of the statues in Westminster Abbey one is of Isaac Watts — frail, sickly, gentle-mannered literary genius of the early eighteenth century. Another is of George Frederick Handel — massive, robust, and hot-tempered master of the keyboard and opera. Both men lived in London. Each knew the other. But neither suspected that their talents would be combined to produce one of the greatest of Christmas carols.

It was in 1719 that pockmarked five-foot little Isaac Watts sat under his favorite tree on the Abney Estate near London and wrote a hymn based on the 98th Psalm. He was 45 years old and had written, among 650 other notable hymns, "Alas, and Did My Saviour Bleed?", "O God, Our Help in Ages Past," and "When I Survey the Wondrous Cross." But the little bachelor's health had broken while he was preaching at London's Mark Lane Church and Lord Mayor Abney carried him out to his estate for a week's rest. That was in 1712, and he was still there writing childs' verse, hymns, and books on a dozen different subjects.

Twenty-two years after Watts wrote his hymn on the 98th Psalm and published it in his "Psalms of David Imitated," a big, fat theatrical producer knelt in prayer in another part of London. He was George Frederick Handel, and he had written some of the world's greatest operas. As a boy in Germany, Handel had persuaded his father to let him study music instead of law and wound up playing a church organ in England. And when he later cast his talents with the theater he carried his religious training with him. At 56 Handel wanted to do something big. And he did. Rising from his knees in 1741 he worked and prayed almost continuously for twenty-three days and nights and came up with his immortal "The Messiah." It was such a masterpiece that for two centuries it has been drawn on as the basis for numerous compositions.

Little Isaac Watts died on the Abney Estates in 1748 after extending his visit of a week to thirty-six years. He was buried in Bunhill Fields, but a statue of him was placed in the Poets' corner of The Abbey, where a statue stands to the memory of a theatrical genius who never forgot God.

It was in 1836 that Boston's choir-director-composer Lowell Mason rearranged a portion of Handel's "Messiah" to fit the hymn Isaac Watts wrote in 1719. And so, while the big statue and the little statue stand as mute reminders of two geniuses in their respective fields, tribute is paid both every Christmas to the resounding echoes of:

JOY TO THE WORLD

By Isaac Watts, 1674–1748

Joy to the world! the Lord is come;
Let earth receive her King;
Let every heart prepare Him room,
And heaven and nature sing.

Joy to the earth! the Saviour reigns;
Let men their songs employ;
While fields and floods, rocks, hills and plains
Repeat the sounding joy.

No more let sins and sorrows grow,
Nor thorns infest the ground;
He comes to make His blessings flow
Far as the curse is found.

He rules the world with truth and grace,
And makes the nations prove
The glories of His righteousness,
And wonders of His love.

9

A Hymn That Was Written
by a Dying Man

A frail man walked feebly down the gangplank. Before he left Northampton he told a group of friends that he could go to heaven from Portugal as well as from England. He had worked too hard and the lung trouble that had plagued him for years had grown worse. So he had come to Lisbon to die.

Philip Doddridge was the last of twenty childen by his London oil-merchant father and pious Dutch mother. As a child he was so frail that his parents feared he would not live. But it was the other way around. Before Philip finished grammar school he lost both his parents. But the mother left her weakling son a heritage that was not only to shape his destiny but was to resound across two centuries.

As a child Philip Doddridge sat on his mother's knee while she told him stories from the Bible. Around the family fireplace were tile decorations representing Biblical events. There was Noah and his ark, Eve's apple and the serpent, Peter crossing the Sea of Galilee, and others. She explained all of these and told Philip of how her own father had been driven from his home by religious persecution. And there on his mother's knee Philip Doddridge "fixed his choice" to follow in the footsteps of his grandfather.

It was an age of religious controversy and a minister was either for the Established Church or he was with the dissenters. But the mild-mannered Doddridge drew the admiration of both. His one great failing was that he ignored his frail constitution. While pastor of Northampton's Congregational Church he took on added duties of running an Academy where he trained 200 young men for the ministry and wrote no less than four hundred hymns. On his travels he carried a manuscript in his saddlebag and even while he shaved a student read to him.

But at 49 tuberculosis forced his hand. Friends advised the drier climate of Portugal and he went there in 1751. But he had waited too long. Three weeks after arriving in Lisbon Doddridge died, and they

buried him there in the English cemetery. Four years later his hymns were collected and published. Among them is this favorite that was sung a hundred years before an unknown writer added the chorus in 1854.

O HAPPY DAY

By Philip Doddridge, 1702–1751

O happy day that fixed my choice
On Thee, my Saviour and my God!
Well may this glowing heart rejoice,
And tell its raptures all abroad.

O happy bond, that seals my vows
To Him who merits all my love!
Let cheerful anthems fill His house,
While to that sacred shrine I move.

'Tis done; the great transaction's done!
I am my Lord's and He is mine.
He drew me, and I followed on,
Charmed to confess the voice divine.

REFRAIN
Happy day, happy day,
When Jesus washed my sins away!
He taught me how to watch and pray,
And live rejoicing every day.

An Immortal Hymn Comes Out of Heated Argument

Perhaps the most popular of the legends about the writing of "Rock of Ages" has as its theme a wandering poet who — caught in a storm and finding refuge under a cleft rock — writes his sentiments while the elements rage. The trouble with the story is that it wasn't invented until seventy-five years after the hymn was written. Actually, the song was born in a less dramatic setting — an argument between two preachers.

"Arminianism" and "Calvinism" mean little to the layman. But those were fighting words to the theologian of two hundred years ago. "Prizefighter" and "chimney sweep" were the terms hurled by Arminian John Wesley at Calvinist August Toplady after the latter had accused the founder of Methodism of acting like a "lurking, sly assassin." Thus the battle went, as both men, sincere in their beliefs, carried on their fight in tracts, sermons, and even hymns — Wesley contending that man could live without sinning and that Grace was free to all, Toplady arguing that everybody was born damned and redemption was a matter of God's choice.

Moving to London as minister to French Calvinists, Toplady became editor of *The Gospel Magazine*. Thus the champion of Calvinism had a new outlet for his arguments. In March, 1776, he wrote an article on "spiritual improvement" and the "National Debt" in which he sought to prove that man was as helpless to pay his debt of sin as England was to liquidate her hopeless national debt. At one sin per second, he figured a man would have chalked up 1,576,800,000 transgressions at the age of fifty . . . but such a staggering debt had already been paid by Christ . . . so "Pray afresh to God."

As was the custom of ministers in writing their sermons, Toplady climaxed his article with a poem. The phrase "Rock of Ages" came from the Bible but it is interesting to note that Wesley had published a hymn 30 years earlier with the opening line, "Rock of Israel, cleft for me."

The Reverend Toplady died at 38, two years after writing his article, and John Wesley was still preaching his theology when he passed on at 88. But it is gratifying that "Rock of Ages" has outlived the age of heated arguments on theology in which it was born, under the lengthy title, "A Living and Dying Prayer for the Holiest Believer in the World."

ROCK OF AGES

By August Toplady, 1740–1778

Rock of Ages, cleft for me,
    Let me hide myself in Thee;
Let the water and the blood,
    From Thy wounded side which flowed,
Be of sin the double cure,
    Save from wrath and make me pure.

Not the labors of my hands
    Can fulfill Thy law's demands;
Could my zeal no respite know,
    Could my tears forever flow,
All for sin could not atone;
    Thou must save, and Thou alone.

Nothing in my hand I bring,
    Simply to Thy cross I cling;
Naked, come to Thee for dress,
    Helpless, look to Thee for grace;
Foul, I to the fountain fly;
    Wash me, Saviour, or I die.

While I draw this fleeting breath,
   When my eyes shall close in death,
When I soar to worlds unknown,
   See Thee on Thy judgment throne,
Rock of Ages, cleft for me,
   Let me hide myself in Thee.

John Wesley Overlooks His Brother's Greatest Hymn

It was March, 1788. Eighty-year-old Charles Wesley preached his last sermon at London's City Road chapel. On the 29th, as friends stood around his bed, he sang Isaac Watts' hymn, "I'll Praise My Maker, While I've Breath." Then the old crusader called for pen and paper. He would praise his Maker with yet another hymn.

Returning to England from Georgia in 1736, where he had been secretary to Governor Oglethorpe, Charles Wesley and his brother John started in earnest on their Methodist movement. In half a century John Wesley, six years older than Charles, traveled a quarter million miles and set England afire with 40,000 sermons. Mild-mannered Charles set the Christian world afire with 6,500 hymns. He wrote perpetually. Many was the time "the Sweet Bard of Methodism" stopped at houses along the road and asked for pen and paper that he might set down verses he had written in his mind while riding on horseback from mission to mission. At 30 he wrote "Hark, the Herald Angels Sing." At 39, "Love Divine, All Loves Excelling," and at 41, "O, For a Thousand Tongues to Sing." Hundreds lay in between. Thousands followed.

When pen and paper were brought to his bed Charles Wesley was too weak to write. But he still had breath and, as his wife took down the lines, he began "In age and feebleness extreme. . . . " His last song on paper, he said "I'll praise . . . " and died.

Publishing a selection of his brother's works, John Wesley pleaded in the foreword of his "Collection" that critics not "tinker" with the poems as "they are really not able to mend either the sense or the verse." But his plea was ignored and even "Jesus, Lover of My Soul" was "tinkered" with for a hundred years before critics conceded that the original could not be improved upon.

Here are four stanzas of the hymn that Henry Ward Beecher said he would rather have written "than have the fame of all the kings that ever sat upon the earth." Many nice stories have been invented about

its writing — birds flying through windows for refuge under Wesley's coat, storms at sea, the author fleeing from mobs, etc. Charles Wesley was simply praising his Maker when, at 31, he wrote his crowning masterpiece. But, strange, John Wesley thought so little of it that it was not included in a Methodist hymnal until Charles had been dead nine years.

JESUS, LOVER OF MY SOUL

By Charles Wesley, 1707–1788

Jesus, Lover of my soul,
  Let me to Thy bosom fly,
While the nearer waters roll,
  While the tempest still is high!
Hide me, O my Saviour hide,
  Till the storm of life is past;
Safe into the haven guide,
  O receive my soul at last.

Other refuge have I none;
  Hangs my helpless soul on Thee;
Leave, O leave me not alone,
  Still support and comfort me;
All my trust on Thee is stayed,
  All my help from Thee I bring;
Cover my defenseless head
  With the shadow of Thy wing.

Thee, O Christ, art all I want;
  More than all in Thee I find;
Raise the fallen, cheer the faint,
  Heal the sick, and lead the blind.
Just and holy is Thy name,
  I am all unrighteousness;
False, and full of sin I am,
  Thou art full of truth and grace.

Plenteous grace with Thee is found,
  Grace to cover all my sin;
Let the healing streams abound;
  Make me, keep me pure within.
Thou of life the fountain art,
  Freely let me take of Thee;
Spring Thou up within my heart,
  Rise to all eternity.

The Captain of a Slave Ship
Reads a Book

An old windjammer tied up at Southampton. The captain staggered down the gangplank, paused, and looked back at his ship. Then he disappeared up the ancient cobblestone street.

Captain John Newton was only twenty-three years old, but he had been to sea ever since his pious mother died when he was seven. He had sailed with his sea-captain father, had done a trick in the British navy, had deserted, been caught, put in irons, and whipped in public. Defiant, he signed on the lowest of all craft — a slave ship. Young Newton hardly knew how to read, but he knew the sea and it wasn't long until he was walking the bridge with a whip in one hand and a gun in the other as master of his own slaver.

John Newton wasn't drunk that day in 1748 when he staggered down the plank. He was sick — sick physically, spiritually, and morally. Most of all he was sick of the filthy slave business. On a long voyage from Brazil he had fallen to reading a book called "Imitation of Christ." Then came a storm — a vicious storm that threatened to send him and his ship to the bottom. When the storm calmed he fell to thinking . . . thinking about Christ whom Thomas a Kempis had written about in his book.

Not an Englishman in His Majesty's empire would have dreamed that Captain John Newton would quit the sea for the ministry. But when the Captain paused for a last look at his ship, that's exactly what he had in mind to do.

After sixteen years of self-education, John Newton was ordained and given a little church at the town of Olney. But he never gave up his sea garb. In the sunset of life, as pastor of one of London's greatest churches, Newton walked the pulpit dressed like a sailor, with a cane in one hand and a Bible in the other. But it was while serving his little church at Olney that he wrote:

AMAZING GRACE

By John Newton, 1725–1807

Amazing grace! how sweet the sound,
That saved a wretch like me!
I once was lost, but now am found,
Was blind, but now I see.

'Twas grace that taught my heart to fear,
And grace my fears relieved;
How precious did that grace appear
The hour I first believed.

Thro' many dangers, toils and snares,
I have already come;
'Tis grace hath bro't me safe thus far,
And grace will lead me home.

When we've been there ten thousand years,
Bright shining as the sun,
We've no less days to sing God's praise
Than when we first begun.

A Troubled Poet Prays for His Soul

William Cowper suffered all of his 69 years. Because of a weak constitution he suffered physically; because of uncontrollable melancholia he suffered mentally. He believed that God had doomed his soul beyond redemption. This belief drove him to attempts at suicide, and he was committed to insane asylums four times. He had studied law but could not plead cases because of stage fright, and his speech was impaired by lisping and stammering. Yet, when he had control of his faculties, William Cowper produced poetry that placed him among the foremost of England's literary giants.

The world can thank, among others, the Reverend John Newton — the one-time sailor and slave trader — for bringing out the best in Cowper. While Curate at the town of Olney, Newton gave the poet a home and put him to work. He built him a house in a garden back of the parsonage; there the strange little man played with rabbits and talked with birds. Newton encouraged and collaborated with Cowper in writing hymns for weekly prayer meetings. Thus came into being the famous collection of "Olney Hymns" — which are some of the finest works in English literature.

During the early part of the last century Composer Lowell Mason — who spent his youth as a bank clerk in Savannah — cast about for poems to set to music for his Boston choirs. Among his selection was William Cowper's "There is a Fountain Filled with Blood." The little poet died, still praying for his soul, in 1800. But he wrote hymns that were to carry his name through the ages, among them being:

THERE IS A FOUNTAIN FILLED WITH BLOOD

By William Cowper, 1731–1800

There is a fountain filled with blood,
Drawn from Immanuel's veins,
And sinners plunged beneath that flood
Lose all their guilty stains.

The dying thief rejoiced to see
    That fountain in his day;
And there may I, tho' vile as he,
    Wash all my sins away.

E'er since by faith I saw the stream
    Thy flowing wounds supply,
Redeeming love has been my theme
    And shall be till I die.

Then in a nobler, sweeter song
    I'll sing Thy pow'r to save,
When this poor lisping, stammering tongue
    Lies silent in the grave.

A Baby Girl Is Born to a
Yankee Carpenter

Oliver Holden put down his saw, beat out a few bars of a melody, and picked up his hammer. The 21-year-old carpenter-musician had come to Charlestown from nearby Shirley, Massachusetts, to help rebuild the town after the British had burned it during the Revolution. Though he never had a lesson in music, Holden became famous for composing a welcoming song for George Washington when the General visited Boston in 1789.

One day the carpenter failed to show up for work and friends called at his home to learn the reason. They found him at his organ. He had just become the father of a baby girl, and he had a song in his heart — a song he was putting on paper.

In 1793 Charlestown was rebuilt. Oliver Holden, at twenty-eight, was dealing in real estate, was a member of the legislature, owned a music store, had built a Baptist Church at his own expense, and was up to his neck compiling material for his hymnal *American Harmony*. The ex-carpenter had found some verses in the English periodical *The Gospel Magazine*, but the author had left off his name.

England's Reverend Edward Perronet had preached and written hymns for the Wesley brothers while they were establishing the Methodist Church. But the fiery tempers of John Wesley and Perronet clashed over laws of the church and John Wesley banned Perronet's hymns from his hymnals. But Perronet kept on writing — under pen names and under no name at all. Oliver Holden didn't know all that. He just knew the anonymous words he found in the magazine matched the tune he had written after his little daughter was born, and the phrase "Crown Him Lord of All" suggested the title "Coronation." But, perhaps, John Wesley wouldn't object because one of the favorite hymns of the Methodists is Edward Perronet's words to carpenter Oliver Holden's tune:

All Hail the Power

By Edward Perronet, 1726–1792

All hail the power of Jesus' name!
Let angels prostrate fall;
Bring forth the royal diadem,
And crown Him Lord of all.

Ye chosen seed of Israel's race,
Ye ransomed from the fall,
Hail Him who saves you by His grace,
And crown Him Lord of all.

Let every kindred, every tribe,
On this terrestrial ball,
To Him all majesty ascribe,
And crown Him Lord of all.

O that with yonder sacred throng
We at His feet may fall!
We'll join the everlasting song,
And crown Him Lord of all.

The Oldest Surviving American Hymn

To avoid confusion, there were two men named Timothy Dwight — both were clergymen, both New Englanders, both Yale presidents. The hymn writer headed the institution from 1795 to 1817. The second changed the college to a university and was its president from 1886 to 1899.

Just as Stonewall Jackson held prayer meetings in his classrooms at Virginia Military Institute, so did Timothy Dwight hold revivals in the chapel of Yale. And for good reason. It was an era when everybody was reading Tom Paine's "Age of Reason," and interviews with students revealed a total of only five professed Christians. So President Dwight took to the chapel pulpit and put the fear of God into his pupils.

Like Benjamin Franklin, Timothy Dwight was one of those sturdy early Americans who could do a good job of almost anything. He was a farmer, clergyman, editor, poet, legislator, orator, businessman, teacher, and educator. As one of his pupils put it, he was interested in "everything" and his knowledge was "boundless." But Dwight's chief interest was in advancing learning and Christianity. An avid Federalist, his chief hate was Thomas Jefferson's doctrine of democratic government. In a Fourth of July oration in 1800 the educator wailed that mankind was being driven back to a savage state and the country was being run by "blockheads."

While teaching Oratory, Literature, and Theology, preaching to his students, and managing the business of Yale, Dwight also took on the editing of a collection of Isaac Watts' hymns. Though his eyes were weak from smallpox and overwork, he wrote thirty-three of his own. Thirty-two have been forgotten but one stands out as the only hymn written in America during the two centuries after the Pilgrims landed on Plymouth Rock that is still in common use.

In addition to making Christians of a spiritually confused student body, Timothy Dwight is best remembered for making these things: a leading institution of a small college, hell for Jeffersonian Democrats, and a hymn that promises to live as long as either Yale or the Party:

I LOVE THY KINGDOM, LORD

By Timothy Dwight, 1752–1817

I love Thy kingdom, Lord,
    The house of Thine abode,
The Church our blest Redeemer saved
    With His own precious blood.

I love Thy Church, O God!
    Her walls before Thee stand,
Dear as the apple of Thine eye,
    And graven on Thy hand.

For her my tears shall fall;
    For her my prayers ascend;
To her my cares and toils be given,
    Till toils and cares shall end.

Beyond my highest joy
    I prize her heavenly ways,
Her sweet communion, solemn vows,
    Her hymns of love and praise.

Sure as Thy truth shall last,
    To Zion shall be given
The brightest glories earth can yield,
    And brighter bliss of heaven.

A Humble Clergyman Is Richer Than His King

The drayman stopped his cart at the little Baptist parsonage at Wainsgate, England. Pushing through a crowd, he started loading the few household goods of the Reverend John Fawcett. After seven years, the 32-year-old minister was moving to London.

Left an orphan at twelve, John Fawcett had worked fourteen hours a day in a sweat shop. He had learned to read by candlelight and had studied hard. Ordained at twenty-five, he had taken the little church with its hundred members for a salary of a hundred dollars a year — to be paid partly in potatoes and wool. Now he was answering a call to London's great Carter's Lane Church.

John Fawcett was to become one of the Empire's greatest scholars and preachers. He was to publish a volume of hymns, write books, and found a school for young preachers. His "Essay on Anger" was to so impress King George III that the Monarch was to offer him "any benefit a king could confer."

The last article was loaded on the cart. The minister started his round of good-byes. There were the young he had married, the children he had held upon his knee, the old whose sorrows he had shared. Few of them could read or write, but their devotion was too much for him. He told the drayman to unload. He would stay a little longer. His stay ended 54 years later. He died there in 1817.

Declining the offer from the throne, John Fawcett said he "needed nothing a king could supply" so long as he could live among the people he loved — the simple people of Wainsgate whose devotion inspired him to write:

BLEST BE THE TIE THAT BINDS

By John Fawcett, 1740–1817

Blest be the tie that binds
    Our hearts in Christian love;
The fellowship of kindred minds
    Is like to that above.

Before our Father's throne,
    We pour our ardent prayers;
Our fears, our hopes, our aims are one,
    Our comforts and our cares.
We share our mutual woes,
    Our mutual burdens bear;
And often for each other flows,
    The sympathizing tear.

When we asunder part,
    It gives us inward pain;
But we shall still be joined in heart,
    And hope to meet again.

A Cabinetmaker Takes Up Writing

"On Christ, the solid rock, I stand; all other ground is sinking sand." That line ran over and over like a refrain in the mind of a 34-year-old London cabinetmaker as he walked up Holborn Hill toward his shop. Edward Mote was happy. He had learned his trade, had worked at it for wages, and now he ran a woodworking business of his own.

Mote spent his few spare hours writing articles for London periodicals. And, now and then, when a key line would hit him, he even tried his hand at writing verse. But most of all Edward Mote was happy because his once confused mind was settled on his belief in God. He had been brought up in a home where the Bible was not permitted and his playground had been the streets of London. But after he became a man he attended Tottenham Court Road Chapel, where sermons of the renowned John Hyatt set his mind at ease.

Edward Mote's cabinet shop ran itself that day in 1834. He had a theme for a poem and he wanted to get it on paper while he had the inspiration. Closeted in his little office, he wrote the caption "Gracious Experience of a Christian" and, as he put it, "In the day I had four verses complete and wrote them off."

The following Sunday Mote went to the home of a minister friend whose wife was near death. Groping for consoling words, the cabinetmaker thought of his verses. He sang them for the dying woman and, at the conclusion of each verse, added the line "On Christ, the solid rock, I stand; all other ground is sinking sand." It was only then that Edward Mote realized he had written a hymn. He had a thousand copies printed for friends, a hymnal picked it up, and "The Solid Rock" has been sung ever since.

Mote gave up his cabinet business, entered the Baptist ministry, and at 55 built a church at his own expense. When his congregation offered to deed the property to him he said, "I only want the pulpit; and when I cease to preach Christ, turn me out of that." At 77, in 1874, he looked up at friends at his bedside and said, "The truths I have preached will do to die upon." And so passed a man who had

been reared in a godless home, learned an honorable trade, and gave it up for the ministry, but whose memory will live for generations because he took time off from his shop one day to write:

On Christ, the Solid Rock, I Stand

By Edward Mote, 1797–1874

My hope is built on nothing less
Than Jesus' blood and righteousness;
I dare not trust the sweetest frame,
But wholly lean on Jesus' name.

When darkness seems to hide His face
I rest on His unchanging grace;
In every high and stormy gale,
My anchor holds within the vale.

His oath, His covenant, His blood,
Support me in the whelming flood;
When all around my soul gives way,
He then is all my hope and stay.

When He shall come with trumpet sound,
Oh, may I then in Him be found;
Dressed in His righteousness alone,
Faultless to stand before the throne.

REFRAIN
On Christ, the solid Rock, I stand;
All other ground is sinking sand.

A Dying Actress Reads the Bible

In 1837 a tall, beautiful woman walked off the London stage, broken in health. When she was five years old her mother had died of tuberculosis. Her only sister had contracted the disease, and now Sarah Flower Adams had played her last role as Lady Macbeth.

Partially regaining her health, Mrs. Adams turned to writing lyric verse, dramatic poems, and hymns, drawing themes for the latter from the Bible. In 1840, when she was 35 years old, the actress was reading the book of Genesis when she came across the story of Jacob at Bethel. Thus was born the theme for what has been called the greatest hymn ever written by a woman. It was among thirteen from her pen to appear in print the following year.

While nursing her sister Eliza, Mrs. Adams broke completely. She lingered two years after her sister died in 1846.

On September 19, 1901, every city in America paused in silent prayer for five minutes — and to sing the assassinated William McKinley's favorite hymn. He had whispered its title as a dying prayer.

"Nearer, My God, to Thee" has rarely been sung since the sinking of the luxury liner *Titanic*, in April, 1912, without associating the hymn with that marine disaster. As the few lifeboats, with their cargo of 600, pulled away, all hope was lost for those left on deck. The ship's band went down playing a composition by Lowell Mason, the dean of hymn-tune writers, as 1,500 helpless souls sang the words of a dying actress who had read the Bible and, like Jacob at Bethel, had a vision of being drawn:

NEARER, MY GOD, TO THEE

By Sarah Flower Adams, 1805–1848

Nearer, my God, to Thee,
Nearer to Thee!
E'en though it be a cross
That raiseth me;
Still all my song shall be,
Nearer, my God, to Thee.

Though like the wanderer,
　　The sun gone down,
Darkness be over me,
．　My rest a stone;
Yet in my dreams I'd be,
　　Nearer, my God, to Thee.

There let the way appear,
　　Steps unto heaven;
All that Thou sendest me,
　　In mercy given;
Angels to beckon me,
　　Nearer, my God, to Thee.

Then with my waking thoughts
　　Bright with Thy praise,
Out of my stony griefs
　　Bethel I'll raise;
So by my woes to be
　　Nearer, my God, to Thee.

Or, if on joyful wing,
　　Cleaving the sky,
Sun, moon and stars forgot,
　　Upward I fly,
Still all my song shall be,
　　Nearer, my God, to Thee.

An Invalid's Mite Becomes a Windfall

The doctor stopped his carriage at the Anglican parsonage in Brighton, England. But there was nothing in his medicine kit to help the paralyzed sister of the Reverend Henry V. Elliott. He was calling to offer his usual word of cheer and to leave one of the little leaflets he had bought to distribute among his shut-in patients.

The leaflets were selling all over England, he said, and were being translated into foreign languages. And for a good cause, too. Someone had written a poem to help finance the building of a school for children of poor clergymen. It said so at the top of the page, "Sold for the benefit of St. Margaret's Hall, Brighton." Under that, the line, "Him that cometh to me I will in no wise cast out." Then came the six-verse poem.

Tears welled in Charlotte Elliott's eyes as she read the lines. Her memory went back to the day her brother had organized a bazaar to start his school and to the thought of how hard he had worked on the project. Everybody in Brighton had helped with the bazaar — that is, everybody except her — a 46-year-old spinster who could hardly get about the room.

Lonely and helpless, Charlotte Elliott had written a poem to console other invalids. She had sent it to a publisher in the hope that from its sale she could contribute a few shillings to her brother's school. And now, her little poem was bringing in more revenue than all the bazaars the town could give.

The doctor was pleased with his call. He had left his patient so happy that she was crying. And the little leaflet must have helped her morale. The following year Charlotte Elliott published a whole book of hymns and she wrote many another before she died at the age of eighty-two. Perhaps the good doctor might have wept a little himself that day in 1834 had he known it was his patient who had written:

JUST AS I AM

By Charlotte Elliott, 1789–1871

Just as I am, without one plea,
  But that Thy blood was shed for me,
And that Thou bidd'st me come to Thee,
  O Lamb of God, I come! I come!

Just as I am, though tossed about
  With many a conflict, many a doubt,
Fightings and fears within, without,
  O Lamb of God, I come! I come!

Just as I am — poor, wretched, blind;
  Sight, riches, healing of the mind,
Yea, all I need in Thee to find,
  O Lamb of God, I come! I come!

Just as I am — Thou wilt receive,
  Wilt welcome, pardon, cleanse, relieve,
Because Thy promise I believe,
  O Lamb of God, I come! I come!

33

An Old Carver Dictates a Poem

Everybody in Coleshill, England, knew William Walford. On Sundays he preached around at different churches for his minister friends. During the week the townsfolk made his little trinket shop their favorite meeting place. Walford was forever whittling out novelties from old bones for children, and he made his scant living carving useful items from ivory. Though his life was filled with adversities and he had seen many "seasons of distress and grief," there was something uplifting about the old carver's pleasant outlook on life.

One day in 1842 when Congregational Minister Thomas Salmon stopped at Walford's shop he found his friend with more on his mind than his carving and his usual optimistic philosophy. The old shopkeeper had composed a poem, and he asked the Reverend Salmon to take the words down as he recited them.

Three years later, on a visit to New York, the Reverend Salmon presented the old carver's poem to the New York *Observer*. It was printed in the September issue of 1845, but nothing of note came of it until fourteen years later. Then, in 1859, a copy of it came to the attention of New York's organist and composer, William Bradbury. Besides directing choirs and writing music Bradbury published some sixty hymn books. He immediately saw in Walford's poem material for a hymn. He set it to music and published it in his *Cottage Melodies*.

The reason William Walford had asked the Reverend Salmon to take down his poem while he dictated it was because he was blind and couldn't see to write.

SWEET HOUR OF PRAYER

By William Walford, 19th Century

Sweet hour of prayer! Sweet hour of prayer!
That calls me from a world of care,
And bids me at my Father's throne
Make all my wants and wishes known;

In seasons of distress and grief,
    My soul has often found relief,
And oft escaped the tempter's snare
    By thy return, sweet hour of prayer.

Sweet hour of prayer! Sweet hour of prayer!
    Thy wings shall my petition bear
To Him whose truth and faithfulness
    Engage the waiting soul to bless;
And since He bids me seek His face,
    Believe His Word and trust His grace,
I'll cast on Him my every care,
    And wait for thee, sweet hour of prayer.

Sweet hour of prayer! Sweet hour of prayer!
    May I thy consolation share,
Till from Mount Pisgah's lofty height,
    I view my home and take my flight;
This robe of flesh I'll drop, and rise
    To seize the everlasting prize,
And shout while passing through the air,
    Farewell, farewell, sweet hour of prayer.

A Sick Preacher Takes a Walk

During the first half of the last century it was not uncommon for the townspeople of Brixham, England, to see a frail, middle-aged man stroll thoughtfully by the seashore. The mild-mannered man was the town's parson and he had taken his daily walks by the sea for twenty years. That was the way he worked out most of his sermons.

But on a Sunday afternoon in September, 1847, the Reverend Henry Francis Lyte took his walk with a heavy heart. He knew it was the last time he would walk the familiar path. When he was 30 years old he had taken the little church at Brixham because he thought the salt air would help his health. Now he was 54, and his lung trouble had grown worse. Doctors said he would have to go to Italy's warmer climate.

At the morning service Lyte had conducted his last sacrament. And now, as he walked beside the sea, he made notes for his farewell message to friends whose joys and sorrows he had shared for nearly a quarter of a century.

In Italy he would be among strangers. But the gentle man knew there was one Friend who would go with him "in life, in death," wherever he went. He put his sentiments on paper and gave the paper to a relative who put it away in a trunk. Lyte died in southern France two months after leaving Brixham. He never reached Italy. In 1861 his poem came to the attention of a London publisher. Composer William H. Monk set it to music: thus was born an immortal hymn.

ABIDE WITH ME

By Henry Francis Lyte, 1793–1847

Abide with me; fast falls the eventide;
*   The darkness deepens; Lord, with me abide;*
When other helpers fail, and comforts flee,
*   Help of the helpless, O abide with me!*

Swift to its close ebbs out life's little day;
*   Earth's joys grow dim, its glories pass away;*
Change and decay in all around I see;
*   O Thou who changest not, abide with me!*

Hold Thou Thy cross before my closing eyes;
*   Shine through the gloom, and point me to the skies;*
Heaven's morning breaks, and earth's vain shadows flee —
*   In life, in death, O Lord, abide with me!*

A Bank Clerk and a Shoe Clerk
Stop for a Chat

Two men stopped in front of a store in Boston. One was Lowell Mason, near middle age and just back from Savannah, Georgia, where for sixteen years he had directed choirs and clerked in a bank. The other was twenty-four-year-old Ray Palmer, recent graduate of Yale and clerk in a drygoods store. Three years later Mason was to be awarded the first degree of Doctor of Music to be conferred by an American college and was to go down in history as the greatest of hymn-tune composers. That same year, 1835, Ray Palmer was to be ordained a minister in the Congregational Church and publish several volumes of verse.

Lowell Mason was one of the busiest men in Boston. He was directing three choirs, hounding the city Board of Education to put a course of music in the schools, and compiling material for his *Spiritual Songs for Social Worship*. That's why he stopped Palmer on the street. He wanted him to write some verses for his new book.

For ten years Ray Palmer had burned the candle at both ends and at times wondered if he could go on. While teaching at a girls' school and studying for the ministry, he almost gave up. One night at his boardinghouse he wrote a poem in a little morocco-bound pocketbook, just to read for renewed courage.

When Mason asked Palmer to write something for his hymnal, the young ministerial student showed him the verses he had carried in his pocket for two years. The composer hurried into a nearby store, borrowed a piece of paper, and copied the poem. Handing the little book back to Palmer, Mason said: "Mr. Palmer, you may do many good things but posterity will remember you as the author of 'My Faith Looks Up to Thee.'" That night in his studio Lowell Mason set to music Dr. Ray Palmer's first and greatest hymn. And Mason was right. Ray Palmer has gone down in history because of that one poem he wrote in his notebook. But, as is the case with many another hymn, Lowell Mason's music played a large part in making it immortal.

MY FAITH LOOKS UP TO THEE

By Ray Palmer, 1808–1887

My faith looks up to Thee,
*   Thou Lamb of Calvary,*
Saviour divine!
*   Now hear me while I pray,*
Take all my guilt away,
*   O let me from this day*
Be wholly Thine!

May Thy rich grace impart
*   Strength to my fainting heart,*
My zeal inspire;
*   As Thou hast died for me,*
O may my love to Thee
*   Pure, warm and changeless be,*
A living fire!

While life's dark maze I tread,
*   And griefs around me spread,*
Be Thou my guide;
*   Bid darkness turn to day,*
Wipe sorrow's tears away,
*   Nor let me ever stray*
From Thee aside.

When ends life's transient dream,
*   When death's cold, sullen stream*
Shall o'er me roll;
*   Blest Saviour, then in love,*
Fear and distrust remove;
*   O bear me safe above*
A ransomed soul!

A Carpenter and the Lord
Write a Hymn Together

Grief fell over the town of Lake Rice, Canada. One of the community's most beloved citizens was dead. Some believed his death was accidental. But the poor people — those who knew him best — wondered if their friend had taken his own life.

Joseph Scriven was born in Dublin in 1820. He was educated on the Emerald Isle and graduated from Trinity College. He was a youth of high ideals, and a beautiful lass had set the day when she would share his high hopes. Then tragedy struck. The day before the wedding the body of the young Irishman's bride-to-be was pulled from a pool of water where she had accidentally drowned.

Scriven never overcame the shock. At twenty-five he migrated to Canada in the hope of forgetting. But he never forgot. For forty years the melancholy man associated himself only with the poor. He worked at simple labor but refused employment from those able to pay. Most of his time was spent sawing wood and doing patch carpentry for widows and the sick.

One day when Scriven was ill an attending neighbor found a poem in his room. Questioned as to the authorship, the modest Irishman replied, "The Lord and I wrote it between us."

Now it was October 10, 1886, and Joseph Scriven was dead. Like his sweetheart of years ago, his body was pulled from a pool of water. Whether he died of his own design really didn't matter. His neighbors built a monument to his memory; not because he had written a famous hymn but because he had devoted his life to the poor.

The poem Scriven said he and the Lord wrote together was:

WHAT A FRIEND WE HAVE IN JESUS

By Joseph Scriven, 1820–1886

What a Friend we have in Jesus,
    All our sins and griefs to bear!
What a privilege to carry
    Everything to God in prayer!

O what peace we often forfeit,
    O what needless pain we bear,
All because we do not carry
    Everything to God in prayer.

Have we trials and temptations?
    Is there trouble anywhere?
We should never be discouraged,
    Take it to the Lord in prayer.

Can we find a friend so faithful
    Who will all our sorrows share?
Jesus knows our every weakness,
    Take it to the Lord in prayer.

Are we weak and heavy-laden,
    Cumbered with a load of care?
Precious Saviour, still our refuge,
    Take it to the Lord in prayer.

Do thy friends despise, forsake thee?
    Take it to the Lord in prayer;
In His arms He'll take and shield thee,
    Thou wilt find a solace there.

A Composer Dodges London Traffic
and Writes a Melody

Composer-minister John Bacchus Dykes could write a melody in a thunderstorm. Of the three hundred hymn-tunes to his credit, many were written in crowded railway stations and on trains. It is said that he wrote some of his best compositions in the pulpit while waiting to deliver his sermons. So neither the rumbling carriages nor clattering hordes of shoppers interrupted his thoughts as he hurried along the streets of London.

John Dykes was running through his mind a poem he had read in an old March, 1834, issue of *The British Magazine*. The lines were under the title, "Faith — Heavenly Leadings," and had been written in June, 1831, by a disturbed Protestant minister named John Henry Newman. Newman had vigorously criticized the Roman church. Then he pondered leaving the Protestant faith for the church he had denounced. By the time he was thirty years old the indecision had shattered his health, and he took a trip to Italy for a rest.

Homesick, stricken with fever, and depressed, Newman waited three weeks for a ship to his native England. When he finally got passage, his ship stopped in the Mediterranean. The sails hung limp on the masts and not a breeze stirred for a week. With the prospect of starving at sea, added to his illness and confused mind, Newman wrote his prayer-poem. He had no thought of its ever being used as a hymn. Two weeks later the ship docked. Twelve years later Newman made up his mind. He went over to the Catholic faith.

When John Bacchus Dykes reached his study that August day in 1865 an immortal hymn was born. But Cardinal John Henry Newman always insisted it was the tune Dykes composed while walking through the busiest section of London that made popular his words:

LEAD, KINDLY LIGHT

By John Henry Newman, 1801–1890

Lead, kindly Light amid th' encircling gloom,
    Lead Thou me on!
The night is dark and I am far from home;
    Lead Thou me on!

Keep Thou my feet;
    I do not ask to see
The distant scene;
    One step enough for me.

I was not ever thus, nor prayed that Thou
    Shouldst lead me on;
I loved to choose and see my path; but now
    Lead Thou me on!

I loved the garish day,
    And, spite of fears,
Pride ruled my will,
    Remember not past years.

So long Thy power hath blest me, sure it still
    Will lead me on
O'er moor and fen, o'er crag and torrent, till
    The night is gone.

And with the morn
    Those angel faces smile,
Which I have loved long since
    And lost a while.

A Governor's Son Discovers a Hymn He Wrote

In the spring of 1865 a young minister took his place in the pulpit of the Second Baptist Church at Rochester, New York. About to preach his trial sermon before a new congregation, he thumbed through a hymnal to select an impressive song. At one page in the book his hand stopped. His eyes widened. Then he smiled. His wife must have played a prank on him. His thoughts went back to a night three years earlier.

It was March 26, 1862. The nation was in turmoil. The War Between the States had swung into its tragic stride. Abraham Lincoln had not yet issued his Emancipation Proclamation and nobody knew what the bloodshed was about, nor where the struggle might end. Everywhere people were praying for Divine guidance. In Philadelphia the son of the Governor of New Hampshire made a talk before a group that had gathered at the First Baptist Church for prayer.

The speaker and his wife went home with Deacon Thomas Wattson for the night. The deacon complimented the young speaker on his selection of a text. Retiring to his room, Joseph Gilmore sat up into the wee hours writing some verse.

The next morning Mrs. Gilmore was up ahead of her husband. She took the paper with its verses but said nothing. Gilmore forgot it completely. Mrs. Gilmore sent the poem to a Baptist periodical. Composer William Bradbury read it, set it to music, and published it in his hymnal, *The Golden Censer*.

At Rochester when Joseph Gilmore, D.D., stopped his hand on a page in the hymnal his thoughts went back to that night in Philadelphia when he talked from the text, "He leadeth me beside the still waters." At any rate, he wanted to hear how a hymn he had written sounded, so he asked the congregation to sing:

44

He Leadeth Me

By Joseph Gilmore, 1834–1918

He leadeth me! O blessed tho't!
O words with heavenly comfort fraught!
What e'er I do, where e'er I be,
Still 'tis God's hand that leadeth me.

Sometimes 'mid scenes of deepest gloom,
Sometimes where Eden's bowers bloom,
By waters still, o'er troubled sea,
Still 'tis His hand that leadeth me.

Lord, I would clasp Thy hand in mine,
Nor ever murmur nor repine,
Content, whatever lot I see,
Since 'tis my God that leadeth me.

And when my task on earth is done,
When, by Thy grace, the victory's won,
E'en death's cold wave I will not flee,
Since God thro' Jordan leadeth me.

REFRAIN

He leadeth me, He leadeth me,
By His own hand He leadeth me;
His faithful follower I would be,
For by His hand he leadeth me.

45

An Author Is Remembered for One Night's Work

During the week the Reverend Sabine Baring-Gould ministered to his little congregation at the mill town of Horbury, England. On Sundays he converted his bachelor quarters into a meetinghouse. At night he held school in the same room. After school he retired to his upstairs bedroom and wrote into the small hours of morning.

Whitmonday was a day of festival for the children of Horbury. And it was the custom for them to march, with crosses and banners, to a neighboring town to join other children for the annual celebration. For the post-Easter event in 1854 the Reverend Baring-Gould was asked to escort the group. On the night before he searched hymnals for a song the children might sing as they marched. Giving up his search, he wrote some verses of his own, wrote over them "Hymn for Procession with Cross and Banners," and went to bed.

That same year the young bachelor saved a mill hand's daughter from drowning, sent her away to school, married her in 1868 — and kept on writing. At the death of his father, in 1881, he inherited a fortune, moved into a mansion at Lew Trenchard — and kept on writing.

For 52 years Baring-Gould wrote a novel a year. He wrote books on religion, mythology, biography, travel, folklore, and theology, and published a book of hymns. His *Lives of the Saints* alone covers 15 volumes. Yet, he wrote all his 85 books in longhand and never had a secretary. "I never wait for an inspiration," he once said, "and when I begin a job I stay on it 'til it's finished."

Had Baring-Gould lived twenty-six days more he would have been 90 when he died in 1924. It is said the literary catalogue of the British Museum lists more titles by him than by any other author of his time. But Sabine Baring-Gould is best remembered for a children's marching song he wrote one night when he was 30 — and which a 29-year-old organist named Arthur Sullivan set to music in 1871:

46

ONWARD, CHRISTIAN SOLDIERS

By Sabine Baring-Gould, 1834–1924

Onward, Christian soldiers,
  Marching as to war,
With the cross of Jesus
  Going on before!
Christ the royal Master,
  Leads against the foe;
Forward into battle,
  See His banners go!

At the sign of triumph
  Satan's host doth flee;
On then, Christian soldiers,
  On to victory!
Hell's foundations quiver
  At the shout of praise;
Brothers, lift your voices,
  Loud your anthems raise.

Like a mighty army
  Moves the Church of God;
Brothers, we are treading
  Where the saints have trod;
We are not divided;
  All one body we,
One in hope and doctrine,
  One in charity.

Onward, then, ye people,
  Join our happy throng,
Blend with ours your voices
  In the triumph song;
Glory, laud, and honor,
  Unto Christ the King;
This thro' countless ages
  Men and angels sing.

47

A Hymn That Was Written by Two Young Men

Henry Smart's father was a violinist and piano maker, and he knew every musician in London. Perhaps that's why the elder Smart put his musically inclined son in law school. But young Henry wanted no part of law. He quit school and was offered a commission in the Indian army, but he declined it. He knew what he wanted. He wanted to be a musician. He meant to be one.

Except for a few lessons by a sympathetic London violinist, Henry Smart trained himself. He worked so intently that by the time he was 23 he had done two things that were to affect the rest of his life. He composed a tune which he called "Lancashire" for the celebration of the 300th anniversary of The Reformation, and he ruined his eyesight.

"Lancashire" was picked up by every tongue from Greenland's icy mountains to India's coral strand and set to words of many a hymn, including Bishop Reginald Heber's "From Greenland's Icy Mountains." The boys at Andover Theological Seminary in Massachusetts were singing the tune in 1888 when they asked their poetically inclined classmate Ernest Schurtleff to write a graduation song just for them. Shurtleff was 26 years old, had graduated from Harvard, and was making a niche for himself in the literary world when he came to Andover to study for the Congregational ministry.

Ernest Shurtleff wrote the song for his class to sing while marching in a body to the ceremony where they were to get their sheepskins. And the tune he borrowed for his verses was "Lancashire," which Henry Smart had written 53 years before.

After serving churches in California, Minnesota, and Massachusetts, Ernest Shurtleff went to Germany and established the American church at Frankfurt. He did relief work during World War I and died in Paris in 1917. When Henry Smart died at the age of 66 in 1879, he was the greatest conductor in England. He had reached his goal but he was totally blind. And, like Ernest Shurtleff, he is remembered best for a job he did while a very young man.

LEAD ON, O KING ETERNAL

By Ernest Shurtleff, 1862–1917

Lead on, O King Eternal,
    The day of march has come;
Henceforth in fields of conquest
    Thy tents shall be our home,
Thro' days of preparation
    Thy grace has made us strong,
And now, O King Eternal,
    We lift our battle song.

Lead on, O King Eternal,
    Till sin's fierce war shall cease,
And holiness shall whisper
    The sweet amen of peace;
For not with swords loud clashing,
    Nor roll of stirring drums;
With deeds of love and mercy,
    The heavenly kingdom comes.

Lead on, O King Eternal,
    We follow, not with fears,
For gladness breaks like morning
    Where'er Thy face appears;
Thy cross is lifted o'er us;
    We journey in its light;
The crown awaits the conquest;
    Lead on, O God of night.

A Revival, a Corn-Shelling Machine, an Accident – a Hymn

"The Work of God in Philadelphia" is what men called the city-wide revival of 1858. Of the participating ministers none was more powerful than the 29-year-old Episcopalian Dudley Tyng. Tyng was a born preacher and had been tutored by his minister father. One Sunday during the revival he stood before 5,000 men in Jayne's Hall. When he pronounced the benediction 2,000 knees were on the floor.

The following Wednesday Tyng was at work in his study. For relaxation he went to his barn to watch a corn-shelling apparatus. The sleeve of his robe caught in a cog, and his arm was torn out of his shoulder. Doctors and a score of ministers gathered at his bedside. The young preacher tried to sing "Rock of Ages," but he was too weak. The Reverend Stephen H. Tyng leaned over to hear the last words of his son who had brought thousands to their knees. "Tell them," the dying young man said, "to stand up for Jesus."

The phrase so impressed Presbyterian Minister George Duffield, Jr., that his next sermon was from the text, "Stand, therefore, having your loins girt about with truth . . . " Then Duffield read a poem he had written. One of his members had the verses printed for distribution in the Sunday School. One of the leaflets found its way to a Baptist periodical. From there it found its way into hymnals and was set to a tune written thirty years earlier by composer George Webb for a secular song. (The same tune is used in the missionary hymn, "The Morning Light Is Breaking.")

In 1864 the Reverend Duffield heard his hymn for the first time when soldiers in a Union Camp sung the verses he had written as a concluding exhortation to a sermon six years earlier.

A revival, a corn-shelling machine, a fatal accident, a hymn, and "The Work of God in Philadelphia" has its influence today.

STAND UP, STAND UP FOR JESUS

By George Duffield, Jr., 1818–1888

Stand up, stand up for Jesus,
    Ye soldiers of the cross;
Lift high His royal banner,
    It must not suffer loss;
From vict'ry unto vict'ry
    His army shall He lead,
Till ev'ry foe is vanquished
    And Christ is Lord indeed.

Stand up, stand up for Jesus,
    The trumpet call obey,
Forth to the mighty conflict,
    In this, His glorious day;
Ye that are men now serve Him
    Against unnumbered foes,
Let courage rise with danger,
    And strength to strength oppose.

Stand up, stand up for Jesus,
    Stand in His strength alone;
The arm of flesh will fail you,
    Ye dare not trust your own;
Put on the gospel armor,
    Each piece put on with prayer;
Where duty calls or danger,
    Be never wanting there.

Stand up, stand up for Jesus,
    The strife will not be long;
This day the noise of battle,
    The next, the victor's song;
To him that overcometh,
    A crown of life shall be;
He with the King of Glory
    Shall reign eternally.

A Preacher Writes a Song for His Sailor Friends

It was April 23, 1888. The Reverend Edward Hopper settled back in the easy chair of his study. The Presbyterian minister had a weak heart and, at 72, was living on borrowed time. But he felt up to writing, so he took a pencil and paper and started outlining a hymn. Nobody knows how many hymns the modest minister wrote because he rarely signed them and when he did he usually used pen names.

During the week days the Reverend Hopper worked among the sailors. On Sundays he preached to them at New York harbor's "Church of the Sea and Land." But when he cast his bread upon the waters through his hymn writing, he always stayed in the background.

Edward Hopper was a man of the city. He was born and educated in New York and, after pastorates at Greenville, New York, and Sag Harbor, Long Island, he was elected to the church at the harbor with its congregation of sailors. Like Methodist Charles Wesley, who often wrote hymns to fit his various congregations, Hopper wrote for the men who go out to sea in ships — "They Pray the Best Who Pray and Watch" and "Wrecked and Struggling in Mid-Ocean." In 1871 one of his hymns was published in *The Sailor's Magazine;* and Philadelphia's sick composer, John Edgar Gould, set it to music the night before he sailed for Africa to mend his health. When it was learned that Gould had died in Algiers, the sailors mourned the death of the man who had set "Jesus, Saviour, Pilot Me" to music. But none of Hopper's own congregation knew their pastor had written the words.

When they found Edward Hopper he was still seated in his easy chair. The pencil was in his hand and a sheet of paper with the outline of a hymn was on the floor. The title was "Heaven," but there was no name of the author. Even if the hymn had been finished, it is doubtful anybody would have known who wrote it. The sailors' hymn was sung nine years before anybody knew Edward Hopper wrote:

Jesus, Saviour Pilot Me

By Edward Hopper, 1816–1888

Jesus, Saviour, pilot me
Over life's tempestuous sea;
Unknown waves before me roll,
Hiding rocks and treacherous shoal;
Chart and compass come from Thee,
Jesus, Saviour, pilot me.

As a mother stills her child,
Thou canst hush the ocean wild;
Boisterous waves obey Thy will,
When Thou sayest to them, "Be still!"
Wondrous Sovereign of the sea,
Jesus, Saviour, pilot me.

When at last I near the shore,
And the fearful breakers roar
'Twixt me and the peaceful rest,
Then, while leaning on Thy breast,
May I hear Thee say to me,
"Fear not, I will pilot Thee."

A Busy Youth Writes a Song
in Half an Hour

Samuel Francis Smith was always busy — always on the go. Just like Lowell Mason, who was forever buzzing about Boston composing music, publishing songbooks, and directing choirs.

It was early in 1832 that civic-minded William C. Woodbridge gave Mason a batch of songs he had brought back from Germany. Woodbridge had picked the numbers up while studying European school systems and thought Mason might translate some of them for his choirs. The music showed promise, but to Mason the words might as well have been written in Egyptian symbols. Then he remembered young Smith, the ministerial student and Harvard graduate who knew fifteen languages.

Samuel Smith lived in the shadow of the church where they hung the lantern the night Paul Revere made his ride. So he naturally absorbed his share of patriotism. It was, according to Smith's account, a half hour before sundown February 2, 1832, that he got around to translating one of the German songs for Mason, not realizing it was the same tune England had been using as its national anthem, "God Save the King." But why the German verses? Why not verses of his own? By sundown his work was done. The following July 4th, Mason's children's choir sang "My Country, 'Tis of Thee" in a Boston park.

On November 16, 1895, a famous Baptist minister hurried to catch a train. He was on his way to fill a preaching engagement. Besides writing books, teaching languages at Newton Center, and holding important posts in his denomination, he was the author of 150 church hymns. The conductor was about to sing out his traditional "board." But he lowered his arm. Something had happened on the platform of one of the coaches. Perhaps the old gentlemen had taken the steps too spryly for his 87 years. At any rate, Samuel Francis Smith died as he had lived — on the go.

Of all his work, Dr. Smith is best remembered for his missionary

54

hymn, "The Morning Light is Breaking," and for some verses he wrote
on a scrap of paper in half an hour when he was 24 years old:

MY COUNTRY, 'TIS OF THEE

By Samuel Francis Smith, 1808–1895

My country, 'tis of thee,
*   Sweet land of liberty,*
Of thee I sing;
*   Land where my fathers died,*
Land of the Pilgrim's pride,
*   From every mountain side,*
Let freedom ring!

My native country, thee,
*   Land of the noble free,*
Thy name I love;
*   I love thy rocks and rills,*
Thy woods and templed hills,
*   My heart with rapture thrills,*
Like that above.

Let music swell the breeze,
*   And ring from all the trees,*
Sweet freedom's song;
*   Let mortal tongues awake,*
Let all that breathe partake,
*   Let rocks their silence break,*
The sound prolong.

Our father's God to Thee,
*   Author of liberty,*
To Thee we sing;
*   Long may our land be bright,*
With freedom's holy light,
*   Protect us by Thy might,*
Great God, our King!

A Priest Goes to a Christmas Play

It was the custom in Austria for roving groups of amateur actors to give plays in the mountain villages. Because the organ in the little church at Oberndorf was broken and the mechanic from nearby Salzburg had parts all over the floor, a local shipowner allowed the annual Christmas play to be given at his home. And, of course, Father Joseph Mohr was invited to see the show.

The sincerity of the young actors touched the priest. After the play he went to the top of a hill that overlooks the tiny village. Alone, he pondered the wonders of the universe. It was a still, clear night — a silent night.

The next morning Mohr called at the home of Franz Gruber. Besides being schoolmaster, Gruber played the church organ — when it was in playing condition. Mohr handed Gruber a carol he had written. He might have it as a Christmas present — and shyly suggested that he try his hand at setting it to music.

That night, December 24, 1818, Father Mohr went to his little church for Christmas Eve services. The organ fixer was there with apologies for not having completed his job. Franz Gruber was there with his guitar and a melody he had written for Mohr's carol. They were young men, the priest and the musician — 26 and 31 respectively. Neither had written a song before and, so far as is known, neither wrote another.

Gruber called Mohr to his side. He plunked the strings, and the two men sang a new Christmas carol. The organ fixer memorized it. Back in Salzburg he sang it for the Stasser sisters. The famous concert singers added it to their collection of native mountain songs — and started it around the world. Translated, English-speaking countries know it as:

SILENT NIGHT, HOLY NIGHT

By Joseph Mohr, 1792–1848

Silent night, holy night,
  All is calm, all is bright
Round yon Virgin Mother and Child,
  Holy Infant so tender and mild,
Sleep in heavenly peace.

Silent night, holy night,
  Darkness flies, all is light,
Shepherds hear the angels sing,
  "Alleluia! hail the King!
Christ the Saviour is born."

Silent night, holy night,
  Guiding star, lend thy light;
See the eastern wise men bring
  Gifts and homage to our King!
Christ the Saviour is born.

Silent night, holy night,
  Wondrous star, lend thy light;
With the angels let us sing
  Alleluia to our King!
Christ the Saviour is born.

A Frail Young Woman
Visits an Art Gallery

Nearly a hundred years ago — 1858 — a frail young woman of twenty-two sat in an art gallery in Germany. Too delicate to attend school regularly in her native England, Frances Ridley Havergal's father had sent her to visit friends in Düsseldorf.

Exhausted from sight-seeing, Miss Havergal sat, by chance, to rest in front of a painting of Christ on the cross. Over the wreath of thorns she noticed the wording: "This have I done for thee; what hast thou done for me?"

Inspired by the painting, Miss Havergal wrote a few lines of poetry. That night at the home of her friends she threw the scrap of paper into the fire. Then there took place one of those strange incidents that shape the destinies of men. A gust of air blew the paper out onto the hearth.

In England she showed the lines to her father the Reverend W. H. Havergal, a hymn-writer and composer in his own right. He encouraged her to add more verses. Thus began one of the most brilliant careers in hymnology.

Always delicate in health, Frances Havergal died at the age of forty-three. When the physician told her the end was near she said, "Splendid! To be so near the gates of Heaven!"

Her hymns are still sung all over the world — and foremost among them is the one that would have been destroyed but for a gust of air.

I GAVE MY LIFE FOR THEE

By Frances Ridley Havergal, 1836–1879

I gave my life for thee,
My precious blood I shed,
That thou might'st ransomed be,

And quickened from the dead,
    I gave my life for thee,
        What hast thou given for Me?

My Father's house of light,
    My glory circled throne,
I left, for earthly night,
    For wanderings sad and lone;
I left it all for thee,
    Hast thou left aught for Me?

I suffered much for thee,
    More than thy tongue can tell,
Of bitterest agony,
    To rescue thee from hell;
I've borne it all for thee,
    What hast thou borne for Me?

And I have brought to thee,
    Down from My home above,
Salvation full and free,
    My pardon and My love;
I bring rich gifts to thee,
    What hast thou brought to Me?

A Sick Hymn Writer
Sits Up All Night

On the evening of February 4, 1874, a group of ten people gathered at an English home for a going-away party for one of the Empire's most noted hymn writers.

During the evening the poetess took the opportunity to study each member of the gathering. She observed that the happiest of the group were those who had found their respective places in life and were using their talents accordingly. While, on the other hand, the most unhappy were those who had not discovered their talents or, in her opinion, were not using their abilities to the fullest.

Frances Ridley Havergal lived in the belief that her talents were a trust from God and were to be used only as He would have them used. Many another artisan has used his talent as sincerely. It was, in fact, the work of a painter with his version of Christ on the cross that inspired Miss Havergal to write her first notable hymn, "I Gave My Life for Thee."

After the guests had gone the 38-year-old poetess retired to her room. Her observations had led her to a renewed conviction that her gift of writing verse was God-given — and to the theme of one of her greatest hymns. As was the case most of her short life (she died at forty-three), she was ill. But she began to write. At dawn Frances Havergal had completed:

TAKE MY LIFE, AND LET IT BE

By Frances Ridley Havergal, 1836–1879

Take my life, and let it be
Consecrated, Lord, to Thee;
Take my hands, and let them move
At the impulse of Thy love.

Take my feet, and let them be
    Swift and beautiful for Thee;
Take my voice, and let me sing
    Always, only for my King.

Take my love; my Lord, I pour
    At Thy feet its treasure-store;
Take myself, and I will be
    Ever, only, all for Thee.

Take my will, and make it Thine;
    It shall be no longer mine.
Take my heart, it is Thine own;
    It shall be Thy royal throne.

Take my love; my Lord, I pour
    At Thy feet its treasure store.
Take myself, and I will be
    Ever, only, all for Thee.

REFRAIN

Lord, I give my life to Thee,
    Thine forevermore to be,
Lord, I give my life to Thee,
    Thine forevermore to be.

61

Gospel Songs Still Popular
After Nearly a Century

The United States was celebrating its hundredth birthday when a new kind of sacred song dawned on the religious horizon, became immediately popular at campmeetings and revivals, swept across the Atlantic, and circled the globe. Literary critics look down their noses at the words and conservative composers frown at the music, as some did at the works of Stephen Foster whose folk songs started the trend. Nevertheless the gospel song has become as much a part of America as Foster's plantation melodies.

It is interesting to note that more gospel-song writers are identified with Ohio and Pennsylvania than any other states. (Foster, also, was from the latter.) To mention but a few, "The Old Rugged Cross" is from the pen of Youngstown's Salvation Army worker, George Bernard; Cincinnati's Wm. H. Doane set to music "Rescue the Perishing," "Safe in the Arms of Jesus," and "Pass Me Not"; E. O. Excell of "Count Your Blessings" was from Ohio's Stark County; and East Liverpool's Will Thompson wrote "Jesus Is All the World to Me" and "Softly and Tenderly."

From Clearfield County, Pennsylvania, came Philip Bliss with "Let the Lower Lights Be Burning," "Almost Persuaded," "Wonderful Words of Life," and a score of others. Philadelphia's singing Irishman William Kirkpatrick wrote "Lord, I'm Coming Home" and set to music "Jesus Saves." Dwight L. Moody's singer Ira Sankey came from the same state to sing gospel songs and compose music for "The Ninety and Nine." When Bliss died in a railroad wreck in Ohio another Pennsylvanian named James McGranahan took his place and became to Evangelist D. W. Whittle what Sankey was to Moody.

Though Moody was the more famous, Whittle was the more versatile. He not only preached the gospel but, under the pen name of "El Nathan," wrote gospel songs for McGranahan to set to music.

Perhaps the gospel songs present a target for both the literary and the music critic, but for seventy-five years these works have served a useful purpose and some have found a favored place while many a scholarly hymn has faded into oblivion. The day may come when the gospel song will give way to another trend, but among those that promise to be popular when the United States celebrates its second hundredth birthday is James McGranahan's music and El Nathan's words:

There Shall Be Showers of Blessing

By El Nathan (Major D. W. Whittle), 1840–1901

"There shall be showers of blessing";
This is the promise of love;
There shall be seasons refreshing,
Sent from the Saviour above.

"There shall be showers of blessing";
Precious reviving again;
Over the hills and the valleys,
Sound of abundance of rain.

"There shall be showers of blessing";
Send them upon us, O Lord;
Grant to us now a refreshing,
Come, and now honor Thy Word.

"There shall be showers of blessing";
Oh, that today they might fall,
Now as to God we're confessing,
Now as on Jesus we call!

REFRAIN
Showers of blessing, showers of blessing, we need;
Mercy drops round us are falling,
But for the showers we plead.

63

Fanny Crosby's Greatest Hymn
Was Among Her First

Dr. Valentine Mott led the little girl and her widowed mother to the door. The famous New York surgeon had made a thorough examination of the child's eyes, but there was nothing he could do. When Fanny Crosby was six weeks old she had caught cold and a doctor had unwittingly prescribed a mustard poultice for her inflamed eyes. Now she was five years old and totally blind. Her father had died, and neighbors in Putnam County, New York, made up money to send her to the noted specialist. As Dr. Mott turned back into his office Fanny Crosby heard him say, "Poor little blind girl." What the sympathetic doctor didn't know was that the little blind girl was to turn her handicap into an asset. Just three years later she wrote her first verse: "Oh, what a happy child I am, although I cannot see! I am resolved that in this world, contented I will be."

Two decades later the superintendent of New York's Institute for the Blind walked into the office to find his male secretary taking down verse while one of the blind instructors dictated. He warned both against further waste of the school's time. But neither thought they were wasting time and continued the practice. In less than two more decades Fanny Crosby's popular verse had made her famous. Among many others her "Rosalie, the Prairie Flower" and "There's Music in the Air" were set to music by noted composer George F. Root and sold in sheet muisc by the thousands.

When Dr. Mott said, "Poor little blind girl," he didn't know the mind of his patient. Fanny Crosby looked on her blindness as a blessing. Undisturbed by things about her, she said, she could more easily write her poetry. She was forty-four years old when she set aside work on secular songs and turned her prolific pen to the writing of hymns. William Cowper must have been right when he said, "God moves in a mysterious way," because Fanny Crosby wrote over 8,000 hymns!

Nor did the one-time school secretary quit taking down her verse. Grover Cleveland set aside affairs of state many times to take dicta-

tion from his ever-welcome guest at the White House. But, as is the case with many writers, Fanny Crosby's best hymns were among her first. She was in the middle of her long life when in 1868 she wrote what singer Ira D. Sankey regarded as her masterpiece:

PASS ME NOT, O GENTLE SAVIOUR

By Fanny Crosby, 1820–1915

Pass me not, O gentle Saviour,
Hear my humble cry;
While on others Thou art calling,
Do not pass me by.

Let me at a throne of mercy
Find a sweet relief;
Kneeling there in deep contrition,
Help my unbelief.

Trusting only in Thy merit,
Would I seek thy face;
Heal my wounded, broken spirit,
Save me by thy grace.

Thou the Spring of all my comfort,
More than life to me,
Whom have I on earth beside Thee?
Whom in heaven but Thee?

REFRAIN

Saviour, Saviour,
Hear my humble cry;
While on others Thou art calling,
Do not pass me by.

A Blind Woman Takes a Hack Ride

The blind poetess Frances Jane Crosby spent the first half of her 95 years teaching the blind and writing popular ballads that, for the most part, were soon forgotten. But after five years of hymn writing her fame circled the globe.

Settled in her new career, "Aunt Fanny" made a practice of visiting revivals and missions to study the effect of her hymns — and to gather material for new ones. And, having contracted to do three hymns a week for one publisher alone, she needed ideas.

It was a hot night in the summer of 1869 that the little blind woman called a hack and rode from her home in Brooklyn to a mission in the Bowery. Word got around that the author of "Pass Me Not, O Gentle Saviour" was in the audience. She was led to the speaker's platform. After making a talk she stepped down to work among New York's lowest derelicts. From that experience came the inspiration for one of our greatest hymns.

Riding home, Fanny Crosby was oblivious to the clattering traffic. Before retiring she put on paper the words she had written in her mind. The next morning she sent the verses to Composer William Howard Doane in Cincinnati. Doane was a business man who had taken up music as a hobby . . . and the hobby had evolved into a profession. He earned the degree of Doctor of Music and wrote music for many of Fanny Crosby's 8,000 hymns. Here are the words the blind poetess wrote in her mind on that memorable hack ride through the streets of New York in 1869:

RESCUE THE PERISHING

By Fanny Crosby, 1820–1915

Rescue the perishing,
Care for the dying,
Snatch them in pity from sin and the grave;

Weep o'er the erring one;
Lift up the fallen,
Tell them of Jesus the mighty to save.

Tho' they are slighting Him,
Still He is waiting,
Waiting the penitent child to receive;
Plead with them earnestly,
Plead with them gently;
He will forgive if they only believe.

Rescue the perishing,
Duty demands it;
Strength for thy labor the Lord will provide;
Back to the narrow way
Patiently win them,
Tell the poor wanderer a Saviour has died.

REFRAIN

Rescue the perishing,
Care for the dying,
Jesus is merciful,
Jesus will save.

A Prayer Is Answered — and
Fanny Crosby Writes Another Hymn

Among many characteristics of the blind poetess Fanny Crosby, three stand out. She always carried a little American flag. She either held it in her hand or kept it in her bag, and it was buried with her when she died in 1915 at the age of ninety-five. Though blinded in infancy, the petite "Aunt Fanny" (she was Mrs. Alexander Van Alstyne in private life) greeted friends and strangers alike with a cheerful "God bless your dear soul." And, according to her own statement, she never attempted to write a hymn without first kneeling in prayer. If this be true, Fanny Crosby spent considerable time on her knees. She wrote no less than 8,000 songs. So many that critics have said the chief fault with her work lies in that she was too prolific. But none can deny that many "pearls are found among the oyster shells."

Under contract for three hymns a week, Miss Crosby was often under pressure to meet deadlines. It was under such circumstances in 1869 that she tried to write words for a tune Composer W. H. Doane had sent her. But she couldn't write. Then she remembered she had forgotten her prayer. Rising from her knees, she dictated — as fast as her assistant could write — words for the famous hymn "Jesus, Keep Me Near the Cross."

But one day in 1874 Fanny Crosby prayed for more material things. She had run short of money and needed five dollars — even change. There was no time to draw on her publishers, so she simply prayed for the money. Her prayer ended, she was walking to and fro in her room trying to "get into the mood" for another hymn when an admirer called. Greeting the stranger with "God bless your dear soul," the two chatted briefly. In the parting handshake the admirer left something in the hymn-writer's hand. It was five dollars — even change. Rising from a prayer of thanks the blind poetess wrote:

All the Way My Saviour Leads Me

By Fanny Crosby, 1820–1915

All the way my Saviour leads me;
*　What have I to ask beside?*
Can I doubt His tender mercy,
*　Who through life has been my Guide?*
Heavenly peace, divinest comfort,
*　Here by faith in Him to dwell!*
For I know, whate'er befall me,
*　Jesus doeth all things well.*

All the way my Saviour leads me,
*　Cheers each winding path I tread,*
Gives me grace for every trial,
*　Feeds me with the living bread.*
Though my weary steps may falter,
*　And my soul athirst may be,*
Gushing from the Rock before me,
*　Lo! a spring of joy I see.*

All the way my Saviour leads me;
*　Oh, the fullness of His love!*
Perfect rest to me is promised
*　In my Father's house above.*
When my spirit, clothed immortal,
*　Wings its flight to realms of day,*
This my song thro' endless ages;
*　Jesus led me all the way.*

A Hymn That Was Written in Fifteen Minutes

William Howard Doane was one of those versatile individuals who could keep several irons hot at the same time. He was an expert accountant, an inventor with seventy patents to his credit, and president and general manager of a woodworking machinery plant in Cincinnati. He played several music instruments, sang in church choirs, published no less than forty songbooks, wrote 2,300 compositions, and was awarded the degree of Doctor of Music by Ohio's Denison University.

Deeply religious, it was natural that Doane should combine his talents with those of hymn-writer Fanny Crosby. The team grew to understand each other so well that when the composer sent melodies to Miss Crosby in Brooklyn the music often suggested themes for verses. And it worked the other way. Many times Miss Crosby sent verses to Doane in Cincinnati and the words suggested a melody. It was, in fact, Doane's ability to sense the sentiment of Fanny Crosby's words and to compose such appealing tunes for them, that the music itself made popular many of the blind writer's hymns. To mention but a few: "Pass Me Not, O Gentle Saviour," "Near the Cross," "Saviour, More Than Life to Me," "I Am Thine, O Lord," and "Rescue the Perishing."

One day in 1868 Doane took "the cars" for New York on a quick business trip. During the ride a melody kept running through his mind. Concluding his business, the composer hurried over to Brooklyn to leave the tune with his co-worker. He ran it off on the organ and, as he had only 40 minutes to get the cars back to Cincinnati, asked "Aunt Fanny" to mail him words for the music. But Fanny asked Doane to start writing. As fast as the composer could take down the words the blind poetess dictated and, according to her own story, Doane was on his way to the station in fifteen minutes.

Settled on the train, the businessman-composer studied the hastily written verses. Each word fitted perfectly with the melody. Thus was

born a hymn that was sung forty-seven years later at Fanny Crosby's funeral:

SAFE IN THE ARMS OF JESUS

By Fanny Crosby, 1820–1915

Safe in the arms of Jesus,
Safe on His gentle breast,
There by His love o'ershaded,
Sweetly my soul shall rest.
Hark! 'tis the voice of angels,
Borne in a song to me.
Over the fields of glory,
Over the jasper sea.

Safe in the arms of Jesus,
Safe from corroding care,
Safe from the world's temptations,
Sin cannot harm me there.
Free from the blight of sorrow,
Free from my doubts and fears;
Only a few more trials,
Only a few more tears!

Jesus, my heart's dear refuge,
Jesus has died for me;
Firm on the Rock of Ages,
Ever my trust shall be.
Here let me wait with patience,
Wait till the night is o'er;
Wait till I see the morning
Break on the golden shore.

An Artist Takes Time Out to Write a Hymn

In 1880 Mary Artemisia Lathbury was thirty-nine years old. She had spent most of those years writing verse and illustrating stories for children. But in the summer of that year the noted artist-writer of juvenile books sat on the bank of a lake in southwestern New York state and read a book that has been published more than any volume between covers. The story Mary Lathbury read from the Bible was about Christ feeding the five thousand.

Because her father and two brothers were Methodist preachers, Mary Lathbury felt so close to that denomination that when she was thirty-two she put aside her pen and brush and took a job as assistant to the Methodist Sunday School Union's Executive Secretary Bishop John H. Vincent. A year later, in 1874, Vincent founded the famous Chautauqua movement. By 1880 Chautauqua had grown to such proportions that the Bishop opined he needed a Vesper hymn just for Chautauqua meetings. So Assistant Mary Lathbury brushed up on her verse writing and came up with "Day is dying in the West; Heaven is touching earth with rest. . . . " She wrote only two stanzas, but the hymn became so popular that she had to write two more stanzas and a chorus. It became so popular, in fact, that it wasn't long until "Day is Dying in the West" was called "one of the finest hymns of modern times" and published in nearly every hymnal in America.

Mary Lathbury became known as "The Laureate of Chautauqua" and when the organization's Literary and Scientific Circle was inaugurated the lyricist was called on to write a "Study Song for members to sing at their gatherings over the country.

BREAK THOU THE BREAD OF LIFE

By Mary Artemisia Lathbury, 1841–1913

Break Thou the bread of life, dear Lord, to me,
*   As Thou didst break the loaves beside the sea;*
Beyond the sacred page I seek Thee, Lord;
*   My spirit pants for Thee, O living Word.*

Bless Thou the truth, dear Lord, to me, to me,
*   As Thou didst bless the bread by Galilee;*
Then shall all bondage cease, all fetters fall;
*   And I shall find my peace, my all in all.*

Thou art the bread of life, O Lord, to me,
*   Thy holy Word the truth that saveth me;*
Give me to eat and live with Thee alone;
*   Teach me to love Thy truth, for Thou art love.*

O send Thy Spirit Lord, now unto me,
*   That He may touch my eyes, and make me see;*
Show me the truth concealed within Thy Word,
*   And in Thy Book revealed I see the Lord.*

A Poverty-Stricken Youth
Turns Hymn Writer

In 1848 a ragged little ten-year-old boy walked from his log-cabin home in the woods of Clearfield County, Pennsylvania, to the neighboring town of Rome. He had brought a basket of berries to sell so that he might add a few pennies to those he was saving to buy a cheap violin.

While walking the streets in search of a market for his berries, the lad heard strains of strangely beautiful music. He hurried toward the house from which the enchanting sound came. It must be a piano, he thought, because his mother had told him about the sound. The only instrument he had actually heard was the flute his father had whittled from a cane.

Putting his basket on the steps, the boy ventured to the open door. When the lady saw him she abruptly stopped playing. Philip Bliss related in later life that he begged the lady to "please play some more." But the lad was not welcome. He was ordered away and scolded for making tracks on the porch with his dusty feet.

Before he died in a railroad wreck in his thirty-eighth year, Philip Bliss was to write many a song that ladies would play on pianos for countless generations. Bliss usually wrote his own words to his melodies, most of his themes being taken from sermons.

As editor of the highly popular *Gospel Songs,* for which his royalties ran more than $30,000, the boy who had once been denied the luxury of hearing a piano wrote:

WONDERFUL WORDS OF LIFE

By Philip Bliss, 1838–1876

Sing them over again to me,
Wonderful words of Life.
Let me more of their beauty see,
Wonderful words of Life.

74

Words of Life and beauty,
  Teach me faith and duty.

Christ, the Blessed One, gives to all,
  Wonderful words of Life.
Sinner, list to the loving call,
  Wonderful words of Life.
All so freely given,
  Wooing us to Heaven.

Sweetly echo the gospel call,
  Wonderful words of Life,
Offer pardon and peace to all,
  Wonderful words of Life.
Jesus, only Saviour,
  Sanctify forever.

REFRAIN

Beautiful words, wonderful words,
  Wonderful words of Life.

A Composer of Popular Songs Turns to Hymn-Writing

During the late 1850's and early 60's a poor man in his twenties rode about rural Pennsylvania driving an old plug he called "Fanny" and a ramshackle buggy that cost him twenty dollars. But considering that he had to support a wife and Fanny on thirteen dollars a month, his buggy had cost a sizable sum.

His name was Philip Bliss. A gentle, self-trained music master, Bliss had been too poor to afford an instrument, and his first notes were learned on a flute cut from a cane back of his log-cabin home in Clearfield County.

At twenty-six Philip Bliss wrote a song he called "Lora Vale." Lora was such a hit that the Chicago publishing firm of Root and Cady induced him to come to the Windy City and conduct concerts.

But the music master cared little for popular music. He wanted to write hymns and sing the songs of the church. This love led him to an association with Chicago's evangelists D. W. Whittle and Dwight L. Moody. In ten years Philip Bliss was among the foremost gospel singers of the nation. One night he heard Moody tell of a ship-wreck, and he wrote "Let the Lower Lights Be Burning." He attended a service where the preacher said "to be almost saved is to be entirely lost," and he wrote "Almost Persuaded." At thirty-five his royalties were counted in tens of thousands — which he gave to charity.

At the Whittle home in Chicago, Bliss pondered the question that many hymns were written along the theme of man's love for God. He reversed the idea, and one morning while his wife waited for him to come to breakfast he wrote:

JESUS LOVES EVEN ME

By Philip Bliss, 1838–1876

I am so glad that our Father in Heaven
    Tells of His love in the Book He has given;
Wonderful things in the Bible I see;
    This is the dearest, that Jesus loves me.

Tho' I forget Him and wander away,
    Still He doth love me wherever I stray;
Back to His dear loving arms would I flee,
    When I remember that Jesus loves me.

Oh, if there's only one song I can sing,
    When in His beauty I see the great King;
This shall my song in eternity be;
    "Oh, what a wonder that Jesus loves me."

REFRAIN

I am so glad that Jesus loves me,
    Jesus loves even me.

A Gospel Singer Hears a Story

But for his untimely death, the golden-voiced Philip Bliss would have perhaps outrivaled Ira D. Sankey as the greatest gospel singer of the last century. With a start of twenty years over the prolific Fanny Crosby, it is also likely that he would have run the blind poetess a close second as America's foremost modern hymn writer. But the Pennsylvania composer enjoyed less than a decade of success when his life was snuffed out at the age of 38 in a railroad wreck in 1876. Thus Philip Bliss is often referred to as "the lamented Bliss."

Philip Bliss got the themes for most of his hymns from sermons. It was from a sermon by a Reverend Brundage that he got his idea for "Almost Persuaded." While singing for Evangelist D. W. Whittle in Chicago, Bliss heard the preacher tell of a battle during the Civil War. From the message came his theme for "Hold the Fort."

The singer-composer was singing for Dwight L. Moody when the renowned evangelist told the story of a shipwreck. Moody related how passengers were lost because the lower lights along the shore were out and only the large light of the lighthouse was burning. The pilot had his general direction but could not see rocks along the entrance to the harbor. "The Master will take care of the great light," said Moody, "let us keep the lower lights burning."

Once an idea struck the alert mind of Philip Bliss, he worked rapidly — usually writing both words and music. At the next service he sang a new hymn for Moody's congregation:

LET THE LOWER LIGHTS BE BURNING

By Philip Bliss, 1838–1876

Brightly beams our Father's mercy
From His lighthouse evermore;
But to us He gives the keeping
Of the lights along the shore.

78

Dark the night of sin has settled,
  Loud the angry billows roar;
Eager eyes are watching, longing,
  For the lights along the shore.

Trim your feeble lamp, my brother!
  Some poor sailor, tempest-tossed,
Trying now to make the harbor,
  In the darkness may be lost.

REFRAIN

Let the lower lights be burning!
  Send a gleam across the wave!
Some poor fainting, struggling seaman
  You may rescue, you may save.

A Gospel Singer Waits for a Train

One Sunday in the early 1870's a lone man stepped from a train in a small Eastern town. His name was Philip Bliss. After twenty years of improverishment and heartbreaking work, he had risen to the front ranks of America's gospel singers and composers of hymns.

Deeply religious, Bliss never missed an opportunity to attend church. He also had very practical reasons for his interest in sermons. It was from the pulpit that he drew ideas for most of his hymns. Dwight L. Moody had told the story of a shipwreck and Bliss had written "Let the Lower Lights Be Burning." He had heard Evangelist D. W. Whittle tell of a battle during the Civil War and he came up with his famous "Hold the Fort."

Waiting for his connecting train to Chicago, the composer slipped into a church. The preacher was reading from the Acts of the Apostles, "Then Agrippa said to Paul, almost thou persuadest me to be a Christian." During his sermon the Reverend Brundage stated, "To be almost saved is to be entirely lost," and Philip Bliss had the theme for one of his greatest hymns.

A music teacher with an income of thirteen dollars a month at 26, Bliss was earning a fortune from his hymnbooks at 36, and giving the fortune to charity. On December 29, 1876, he and his wife were riding a Chicago-bound express through Ohio. Near the town of Ashtabula the train crashed through a trestle and burned. The composer crawled from the wreckage, but when he could not find his wife he fought his way back through the flames in an effort to find her. He perished with his wife and a hundred other passengers. He would have been 38.

ALMOST PERSUADED

By Philip Bliss, 1838–1876

"*Almost persuaded,*" *now to believe;*
  "*Almost persuaded,*" *Christ to receive;*
Seems now some soul to say,
  "*Go, Spirit, go Thy way,*
Some more convenient day,
  On Thee I'll call."

"*Almost persuaded,*" *come, come today;*
  "*Almost persuaded,*" *turn not away;*
Jesus invites you here,
  Angels are ling'ring near,
Prayers rise from hearts so dear,
  O wand'rer, come.

"*Almost persuaded,*" *harvest is past!*
  "*Almost persuaded,*" *doom comes at last!*
"*Almost*" *cannot avail;*
  "*Almost*" *is but to fail!*
Sad, sad, that bitter wail,
  "*Almost,*" *but lost.*

A Hymn Is Born of a Casual Remark

Like many another temperamental artist, Composer Joseph Webster had his off days. So when he sauntered into the office of Dr. Sanford Bennett, where he usually hung his hat and violin, the doctor knew the musician was in the dumps.

"What's the trouble now?" Bennett asked Webster.

"O, nothing," came the dejected reply. "Everything will be all right by and by."

The doctor turned back to his desk where he wrote prescriptions as a profession and verse as a hobby. "By and by," he mused, "the sweet by and by." He paused, looked up at Webster, then reached for writing paper.

Joseph Philbrick Webster was an out-and-out musician. In the East, where he was born in 1819, he had been an active member of the Handel and Haydn Society and a prolific composer of popular songs. In his early thirties he migrated to Indiana and, in 1857, settled in Elkhorn, Wisconsin. When verse-writing physician Sanford Fillmore Bennett moved to the same town in 1861, the two struck up a partnership in the production of sheet music. After six years of working together Bennett learned Webster like a songbook. He soon found that the best prescription for his partner's spells of melancholia was a batch of verse to be set to music. However, on that autumn day in 1867 the doctor had no remedy on hand. But Webster's casual remark gave him a theme — not for another of their popular songs but for a hymn.

While the physician wrote hastily at his desk, two townsmen joined Webster at the stove. In a few minutes Bennett handed Webster three verses and a chorus. In less time than it had taken the doctor to write the words, the composer had the music. He gave the melody a few rounds on his violin, and the four men sang for the first time:

In the Sweet By-and-By

By S. F. Bennett, 1836–1898

There's a land that is fairer than day,
    And by faith we can see it afar;
For the Father waits over the way,
    To prepare us a dwelling place there.

We shall sing on that beautiful shore
    The melodious songs of the blest,
And our spirits shall sorrow no more,
    Not a sigh for the blessing of rest.

To our bountiful Father above,
    We will offer our tribute of praise,
For the glorious gift of His love,
    And the blessings that hallow our days.

REFRAIN

In the sweet by-and-by,
    We shall meet on that beautiful shore;
In the sweet by-and-by,
    We shall meet on that beautiful shore.

A Preacher and a Singer
Take a Train Ride

Two tired men hurried through the railroad station at Glasgow, Scotland. One of them paused, bought a newspaper, and stuffed it into his pocket. On the train they took seats facing each other. One of the men was Dwight L. Moody, the greatest evangelist of the time. The other was Ira D. Sankey, who sang to his own accompaniment; if not the greatest gospel singer of the past century, he was certainly one of the greatest. The pair had just closed an extended revival in Glasgow and were on their way to Edinburgh for an engagement.

Moody waded into a bundle of unopened letters from his home in Chicago. It was 1874. His church had been destroyed three years earlier in the great fire and he was anxious about progress on his new tabernacle. Sankey scanned his newspaper. He was about to toss it aside when he noticed a poem written by a little orphaned Scotch girl named Elizabeth Clephane. He read the lines over and over. He tore the poem out and put it into his pocket.

In Edinburgh Moody preached on the subject, "The Good Shepherd." Came time for Sankey's solo. The singer had not expected the sermon and had no appropriate number. Then he thought of the poem. He put it on the music rack, his hand hit the keys, and he started singing.

This is, perhaps, the only case in the history of hymn making where a tune was composed — note for note — just as it stands today, while the composer sang it for the first time.

THE NINETY AND NINE

By Elizabeth Clephane, 1830–1869

There were ninety and nine that safely lay
In the shelter of the fold,
But one was out on the hills away,
Far off from the gates of gold.

84

Away on the mountain wild and bare,
  Away from the tender Shepherd's care.

"Lord, Thou hast here Thy ninety and nine;
  Are they not enough for Thee?"
But the Shepherd made answer: "This of mine
  Has wandered away from Me;
And although the road is rough and steep,
  I go to the desert to find My sheep."

But all through the mountains, thunder riven,
  And up from the rocky steep,
There arose a glad cry to the gate of Heaven,
  "Rejoice! I have found My sheep!"
And the angels echoed around the throne,
  "Rejoice, for the Lord brings back His own!"

A Circus Music Master
Writes a Hymn

Elgin is a few minutes' drive from Chicago and Kirkland is a few minutes west of Elgin. It was in Elgin and Kirkland that a forgotten music master and circus performer spent the last days of his 85 years. His name was Daniel A. (Dion) De Marbelle who, in his better years, could do anything — and had done everything.

As a youth Dion De Marbelle sailed from his native France, where he had been born in 1818, to roam the Arctic Ocean on a whaling ship. In 1847 he served with the American Navy in the Mexican War. As actor, singer, and musician he toured the continent. When the North and South clashed in '61 he joined the Federals and played in the Sixth Michigan Infantry band. After Appomattox he went with James A. Bailey's circus as a musician; and when Bailey went with Barnum in 1881 to form "The Greatest Show on Earth," De Marbelle organized his own outfit. Losing his tents and other equipment in a fire in Canada, the aging showman joined Buffalo Bill Cody to organize the famous Wild West Shows.

Old files of the Elgin Daily *Courier-News* recount that the versatile entertainer was an accomplished sleight-of-hand artist, a one-man minstrel show, an eloquent speaker "on any subject," and a poet and composer of popular ballads. On Sundays he sang in the Methodist choir. During the week he called community dances.

In 1887 De Marbelle was nearing three score and ten and he wanted to leave something lasting. And he did. But, as with his more than twenty-five other songs, De Marbelle received not a dollar for "When They Ring The Golden Bells." In December, 1903, the old performer went on to "dwell with the immortals" in the "land beyond the river." Old soldiers of the G. A. R. buried him in Elgin, and the government placed a modest marker at his grave. There is no other tribute — no dates — just the simple wording, "Drum Major D. A. De Marbelle, 6 Mich. Inf."

86

And there in Soldiers' Reserve at the Bluff City cemetery the music master whose artistry thrilled thousands beneath the big top, and who left behind an immortal hymn, awaits the day when "the King commands the spirit to be free."

WHEN THEY RING THE GOLDEN BELLS

By Dion De Marbelle, 1818–1903

There's a land beyond the river,
That we call the sweet forever,
And we only reach that shore by faith's decree;
One by one we'll gain the portals,
There to dwell with the immortals,
When they ring the golden bells for you and me.

We shall know no sin or sorrow,
In that haven of tomorrow,
When our barque shall sail beyond the silver sea;
We shall only know the blessing
Of our Father's sweet caressing,
When they ring the golden bells for you and me.

When our days shall know their number,
When in death we sweetly slumber,
When the King commands the spirit to be free;
Never more with anguish laden,
We shall reach that lovely aiden,
When they ring the golden bells for you and me.

REFRAIN

Don't you hear the bells now ringing?
Don't you hear the angels singing?
'Tis the glory hallelujah Jubilee.
In that far-off sweet forever,
Just beyond the shining river,
When they ring the golden bells for you and me.

87

A President Goes to Church
with His Mother

The spry little woman of 87 smiled proudly at her neighbors. It was Sunday and she was walking to church with her son. He was President of the United States, but she was as proud of him as if he had been a Methodist Bishop.

Everybody knows that William McKinley was devoted to his mother. Everybody knows that he was a devout Christian, taught a Bible class, and was superintendent of a Methodist Sunday School. What everybody does not know is that every day of his mother's life — as lawyer, Congressman, Governor of Ohio, and United States President — when William McKinley did not see his mother he either wrote or telegraphed her.

In mid-October, 1897, McKinley slipped out of the White House and took a train for Canton just to walk to church with his mother. He wanted to walk to church with her like he and his brothers and sisters had when "Mother McKinley" carried her brood to church as soon as they were old enough to toddle at her side.

Nancy Allison McKinley raised five girls and four boys but, somehow, she seemed to lean to her husband's namesake. "William is going to be a bishop someday," she once said proudly. But when William became United States President instead, it was all right with her. He would conduct himself like the Christian gentleman she had raised, whether he be bishop or president.

When President William McKinley's mother became ill in the winter of 1897, he had her home in Canton connected with the White House by special wire and he kept a special train standing by under full steam. One night when "Mother McKinley" called for William, attendants wired, "Mr. President, we think you had better come." The answer flashed back, "Tell Mother I'll be there."

On Sunday afternoon, Dec. 12, 1897, Nancy McKinley breathed her last in the arms of her big 54-year-old son. For fully an hour after she died he didn't move from her bedside.

88

Less than four years later, while making a speech in Buffalo, McKinley was cut down by a bullet from the gun of anarchist Leon Czolgosz. With no bitterness even for his assassin, the dying president said, "God's will be done." Then he called for a hymn his mother had taught him, "Nearer, My God, to Thee." His body was brought back to Canton and laid to rest — beside his mother.

Reading a newspaper account of McKinley's telegram to those at his mother's bedside, hymn-writer Charles M. Fillmore was inspired to write this hymn — using as a title the dramatic message:

TELL MOTHER I'LL BE THERE

By Charles M. Fillmore, 1860——

When I was but a little child, how well I recollect,
How I would grieve my mother with my folly and neglect;
And now that she has gone to heaven I miss her tender care,
O Saviour, tell my mother I'll be there.

Though I was often wayward, she was always kind and good;
So patient, gentle, loving, when I acted rough and rude;
My childhood griefs and trials she would gladly with me share:
O Saviour, tell my mother I'll be there.

One day a message came to me, it bade me quickly come
If I would see my mother ere the Saviour took her home;
I promised her before she died, for heaven to prepare;
O Saviour, tell my mother I'll be there.

REFRAIN

Tell mother I'll be there, in answer to her prayer,
This message, blessed Saviour, to her bear!
Tell mother I'll be there, heaven's joys with her to share,
Yes, tell my darling mother I'll be there.

The Hymn That Was Born
in an Epidemic

People were dying all over New York. An epidemic was sweeping the city, and when the Reverend Robert Lowry wasn't visiting sick members of his Hanson Place Baptist Church he was burying others who had crossed over Jordan. That's why the 38-year-old clergyman was near exhaustion when he flopped down on the couch of his Brooklyn home one hot day in July, 1864. But he didn't stay there long. He got to thinking about all the people who were dying. Then he fell to thinking of the great reunion at the river of life, and soon he was busy writing.

Robert Lowry, D.D., was a preacher. He said that was all he was — a preacher. After his hymns made him famous and he became referred to as a composer, he said he "felt a sort of meanness." Preaching was his business. Hymn writing was a side line and he said he would rather preach a gospel sermon to an attentive audience any day. When asked what method he used in writing both words and music for many of his hymns, he said he had no method — music just ran through his head all the time; and, when he was in the mood, the words came by inspiration — just like that. Unlike Fanny Crosby, who "made" her moods, Lowry waited for his and wrote wherever he was — often on the edges of newspapers or the backs of envelopes.

Judging from his voluminous hymns, preacher Lowry must have had lots of moods before he died at Plainfield, New Jersey in 1899. Who hasn't heard "Where is My Wandering Boy Tonight?" that Lowry wrote for the temperance movement in 1877, or his music to "What Can Wash Away My Sins?"

Exhausted as he was, Dr. Lowry's mood must have been working overtime that sultry afternoon. He reached for a scrap of paper, wrote four verses, and went over to his organ. Before he lay back on his couch he had completed a hymn that has outlived every sermon he ever preached:

SHALL WE GATHER AT THE RIVER?

By Robert Lowry, 1826–1899

Shall we gather at the river,
    Where bright angels feet have trod,
With the crystal tide forever
    Flowing by the throne of God?

On the margin of the river,
    Washing up its silver spray,
We will walk and worship ever,
    All the happy golden day.

Ere we reach the shining river,
    Lay we every burden down;
Grace our spirits will deliver,
    And provide a robe and crown.

Soon we'll reach the shining river,
    Soon our pilgrimage will cease,
Soon our happy hearts will quiver
    With the melody of peace.

REFRAIN

Yes, we'll gather at the river,
    The beautiful, the beautiful river,
Gather with the saints at the river
    That flows by the throne of God.

A Quiet Man Is Heard
Around the World

Visitors were barred from the sickroom. Dwight L. Moody, the evangelist who had stirred fifty million listeners on two continents, had preached his last sermon. A gentleman in his early fifties waited in the hall. It was December, 1899, and cold, but Will Thompson had come to Northfield, Massachusetts, from his home in East Liverpool, Ohio, to pay respects to a man who, with singer Ira D. Sankey, had "reduced the population of hell by a million souls."

Will Lamartine Thompson's gift of music and poetry was matched with "a fine character of sincerity, simplicity, and righteousness." He wrote his first song in 1863 at the age of 16 and ten years later, while studying at Boston's Conservatory of Music, came out with "Gathering Shells by the Seashore." The hit swept the nation from shore to shore and gathered a fortune for the youthful composer, who left for Germany to further his musical education and returned to write "My Home on the Old Ohio" and "Under the Moonlit Sky."

Riding the crest of fame and fortune at forty, the mild-mannered composer-poet turned his back on secular compositions and turned his pen to writing hymns. Thompson opened a music store, set up his own publishing house for church songs, and bought a two-horse wagon. While Sankey with the voice that could be heard a mile was singing to multitudes across America and England, Will Thompson was driving his team of horses in Ohio and singing his own hymns in rural homes. When he found no piano he simply unloaded the one on his wagon and played his own accompaniment to his "Lead Me Gently Home, Father," "There's a Great Day Coming," and "Jesus is All the World to Me." At the same time, penitents by the thousands streamed down Moody's sawdust trail to Sankey's singing of Will Thompson's "Softly and Tenderly Jesus is Calling." The echo swept across South Africa and it was translated in Hawaii.

Through the door of his sickroom Dwight L. Moody heard someone mention the name of Will Thompson. Ignoring doctors' orders

the dying evangelist demanded that his old friend be admitted. Feebly taking the "Bard of Ohio" by the hand the dying Moody said, "Will, I would have rather written 'Softly and Tenderly Jesus is Calling' than anything I have been able to do in my whole life."

SOFTLY AND TENDERLY

By Will Thompson, 1847–1909

Softly and tenderly Jesus is calling,
  Calling for you and for me;
See, on the portals He's waiting and watching,
  Watching for you and for me.

Why should we tarry when Jesus is pleading,
  Pleading for you and for me?
Why should we linger and heed not His mercies,
  Mercies for you and for me?

Time is now fleeting, the moments are passing,
  Passing from you and from me;
Shadows are gathering, deathbeds are coming,
  Coming for you and for me.

Oh! for the wonderful love He has promised,
  Promised for you and for me;
Tho' we have sinned, He has mercy and pardon,
  Pardon for you and for me.

REFRAIN

Come home, come home,
  Ye who are weary, come home,
Earnestly, tenderly, Jesus is calling,
  Calling, O sinner, come home!

A Distraught Woman Inspires the Writing of a Hymn

Burdened with seemingly unbearable sorrow, a despondent woman wrung her hands and repeatedly cried, "What shall I do? What shall I do?" To which a sympathetic minister replied, "You can do nothing better than tell your sorrow to Jesus." Thus was the setting for the writing of one of the greatest of gospel hymns.

When Pennsylvania's Reverend Elisha A. Hoffman was not working on sermons and hymns in his study, he was working with the poor and downcast in homes across the tracks. By standards of large churches, the Evangelical minister was not a great preacher. By standards of a useful life Elisha Hoffman was, like his father, a great minister. It was while serving a church at Lebanon, some thirty miles from the town of Orwigsburg where he was born in 1839, that Hoffman experienced the touching scene that inspired the writing of one of the most popular of his more than 2000 gospel hymns.

While visiting a parishioner's home where "God permitted many visitations of sorrow and affliction," the minister found the woman of the house in the depths of despair. He prayed with her and, as he put it, "I quoted from the Word" such passages as "Come unto me all ye that labor and are heavy laden and I will give you rest." Still the woman frantically wrung her hands and repeated her cries of "What shall I do?" Finally Hoffman suggested that she could do nothing better than "tell your sorrow to Jesus."

As Hoffman left the woman seemed absorbed with her thoughts, her eyes lighted up, and with animation she exclaimed, "Yes, I must tell Jesus!"

"Down at the Cross Where My Saviour Died," "Leaning on the Everlasting Arms," and "Are You Washed in the Blood of the Lamb?" are but a few favorite hymns from the pen of Elisha Hoffman that have echoed across America for half a century. But it was the ringing words of a downcast woman that inspired the writing of one of his greatest. On his way home the phrase "I Must Tell Jesus" kept run-

ning through Hoffman's mind and he went directly to his study, where
he wrote both music and the words: .

I Must Tell Jesus

By Elisha A. Hoffman, 1839–1929

I must tell Jesus all of my trials;
I cannot bear these burdens alone;
In my distress He kindly will help me;
He ever loves and cares for His own.

I must tell Jesus all of my troubles;
He is a kind, compassionate Friend;
If I but ask Him, He will deliver,
Make of my troubles quickly an end.

Tempted and tired I need a great Saviour,
One who can help my burdens to bear;
I must tell Jesus, I must tell Jesus;
He all my cares and sorrows will share.

O how the world to evil allures me!
O how my heart is tempted to sin!
I must tell Jesus, and He will help me
Over the world the victory to win.

REFRAIN

I must tell Jesus! I must tell Jesus!
I cannot bear my burdens alone,
I must tell Jesus! I must tell Jesus!
Jesus can help me, Jesus alone.

A Little Girl Fails to Answer
When Her Name Is Called

James M. Black walked home with a heavy heart. Except for his thoughts he was alone as he made his way along the streets of his native Williamsport, Pennsylvania. Bessie had never failed before to answer roll call at Sunday School. Black knew because he called the roll himself. But when Bessie didn't answer that morning he called her name a second time. Still she didn't answer, and Black knew something was wrong. Then somebody said Bessie had suddenly taken ill and doctors held little hope for her life.

To social worker James Black, Bessie was more than just another recruit for the Sunday School class and Young Peoples' Society. She lived on the other side of the tracks in what was called before the turn of the century "The Sawdust City." He had found the little girl one day sitting on the broken-down steps of a broken-down house. Her clothes were ragged, and folks said her parents thought more of the bottle than they did of Bessie. Of course she would come to Sunday School and she would be there the next Sunday. Then she looked at her clothes and said maybe she couldn't come after all. But the next day somebody left a box of new clothes at Bessie's house and every one of them just fitted. And every Sunday after that when James Black called the roll he looked up and sort of smiled when he came to Bessie's name.

As he walked home that Sunday in 1893 James Black got to thinking that maybe the next time Bessie answered to her name it would be at the great roll call. Then he got to wondering if his own name might be on the same roll.

Besides teaching Sunday School, Black loved to play the piano and write poetry. He said that the words for the hymn just seemed to come to him spontaneously, and he wrote them down that afternoon. That night he set them to music. Black collected his poems into a little book he called *Songs of the Soul*. In the book is the three-verse

poem he wrote just before a little girl named Bessie went on to answer to her name:

WHEN THE ROLL IS CALLED UP YONDER

By James M. Black, 1859–1936

When the trumpet of the Lord shall sound, and the time shall be no more,
*   And the morning breaks, eternal, bright and fair;*
When the saved of earth shall gather over on the other shore,
*   And the roll is called up yonder, I'll be there.*

On that bright and cloudless morning when the dead in Christ shall rise
*   And the glory of His resurrection share;*
When His chosen ones shall gather to their home beyond the skies,
*   And the roll is called up yonder, I'll be there.*

Let us labor for the Master from the dawn till setting sun,
*   Let us talk of all his wondrous love and care;*
Then when all of life is over, and our work on earth is done,
*   And the roll is called up yonder, we'll be there.*

REFRAIN

When the roll is called up yonder,
*   When the roll is called up yonder,*
When the roll is called up yonder,
*   When the roll is called up yonder, I'll be there.*

A Father's Singing
Inspires His Son

Johnson Oatman, Sr., had a rich, powerful voice. To people of the town of Lumberton, their local merchant was the best singer in New Jersey. That's why Johnson Oatman, Jr., always sat next to his father in church. He loved church music, and he loved to hear his father sing. Perhaps that is why Johnson Oatman, Jr., grew into manhood with a fervent desire to contribute something to the faith of his father.

As junior member of the firm of Johnson Oatman & Son young Oatman found little outlet for his religious ambitions. So he studied for the Methodist ministry and was ordained. But the limits of one church narrowed his horizons, and he went from pulpit to pulpit as a "local preacher." Still he had not hit upon his true calling. But when he was 36 years old, Johnson Oatman, Jr., found his talent. If he could not sing like his father he could write songs for others to sing. He found a channel with no limits, and he could preach to millions through sermons in song.

It was in 1892 that Johnson Oatman, Jr., picked up his pen. Three years later the world was singing, among scores of others, "There's not a friend like the lowly Jesus, no not one, no not one." In 1898 presses rolled off a favorite that is found in hymnals around the globe — his inspiring "Higher Ground."

It was in 1897 that Oatman wrote what critics regard as his masterpiece. Composer E. O. Excell of Stark County, Ohio, set "Count Your Blessings" to music; and of this number Evangelist Gypsy Smith once said, "Men sing it, boys whistle it, and women rock their babies to sleep to the tune." And so he wrote. Two hundred gospel hymns came from his pen every year for a quarter of a century. The total passed 5,000. When publishers required that Oatman set a price on his work, it is said that he declined to accept more than one dollar per song.

Johnson Oatman, Jr., died at Mount Pleasant, New Jersey, in

1926. He was never a great preacher. He never sang like his father.
But he found his talent and he made his contribution. And he still
preaches to millions every year through such songs as:

COUNT YOUR BLESSINGS

By Johnson Oatman, Jr., 1856–1926

When upon life's billows you are tempest-tossed,
When you are discouraged, thinking all is lost,
Count your many blessings, name them one by one,
And it will surprise you what the Lord hath done.

Are you ever burdened with a load of care?
Does the cross seem heavy you are called to bear?
Count your many blessings, ev'ry doubt will fly,
And you will be singing as the days go by.

So, amid the conflict, whether great or small,
Do not be discouraged, God is over all;
Count your many blessings, angels will attend,
Help and comfort give you to your journey's end.

REFRAIN

Count your blessings, Name them one by one;
Count your blessings, See what God hath done;
Count your blessings, Name them one by one;
Count your many blessings, See what God hath done.

A Hymn That Was Inspired
by a Prayer

The railroad station was crowded. It was just before Christmas, and it seemed that everybody in New York was going somewhere. Nobody noticed the little lady as she modestly made her way to the window and bought a ticket. Nobody noticed her as she quietly watched the milling throngs while she waited for her train to be called. But that's the way she wanted it. She didn't like to be noticed. However, traveling was nothing new to her. As a Bible teacher and Christian worker she had been all over the United States, had spent several years in England and, when she was nearly 60, had made a trip to Africa. So there she was, past three score and ten, waiting for another train. This time to fill an engagement down in Philadelphia.

Adelaide Pollard was a remarkable little woman. She devoted all of her life to making the world a better place, but she didn't want any recognition for it. Nobody knows how many hymns she wrote because she rarely signed them, and when she did she just put the initials "A. A. P." That's why if you look up "Have Thine Own Way, Lord" in your hymnal, the chances are you will see only "A. A. P." at the left under the title.

Miss Pollard had just passed 40 at the turn of the century when she got the inspiration to write "Have Thine Own Way." She was at a prayer service when an elderly woman used a phrase that struck her. In her prayer the woman omitted the usual request for blessings, but prayed simply that the Lord "just have your own way with our lives." The sincerity of the prayer so impressed Miss Pollard that by the time she got home that night she had the hymn shaped in her mind and put it on paper before she went to bed.

Perhaps The Great Conductor figured Adelaide Pollard had done enough traveling on earth. The caller announced the train for Philadelphia that day in December, 1934, but the quiet little lady of 72 didn't get on it. The throngs milled through the gate, but the author of "Have Thine Own Way, Lord" was called to keep an appointment

with God. They buried her at Fort Madison in her native state of Iowa.

HAVE THINE OWN WAY, LORD

By Adelaide Pollard, 1862–1934

Have Thine own way, Lord!
Have Thine own way!
Thou art the Potter,
I am the clay.
Mould me and make me
After Thy will,
While I am waiting,
Yielded and still.

Have Thine own way, Lord!
Have Thine own way!
Search me and try me,
Master today!
Whiter than snow, Lord,
Wash me just now,
As in Thy presence
Humbly I bow.

Have Thine own way, Lord!
Have Thine own way!
Wounded and weary,
Help me, I pray!
Power — all power —
Surely is Thine!
Teach me and heal me,
Saviour divine!

Have Thine own way, Lord!
Have Thine own way!
Hold o'er my being
Absolute sway!
Fill with Thy Spirit
Till all shall see
Christ only, always,
Living in me!

The Hymn That Was Taken
from the Dictionary

"God be with you" is what the dictionary gives as definition of the phrase "good-by." And that's how Jeremiah Rankin got the theme for his famous benediction hymn. The minister of Washington's First Congregational Church wanted to write a song for the conclusion of Christian gatherings, so he looked in the dictionary for the meaning of "good-by," found that it said, "A condensation of 'God be with you,'" and started writing his hymn just like that. "It was," said Dr. Rankin, "called forth by no person or occasion."

That was in 1880. The 52-year-old minister sent the first verse over to organist William G. Tomer at Grace Methodist Episcopal Church. Tomer, one-time schoolteacher, writer, and clerk in the Treasury Department, set the verse to music, and sent it back. Rankin's church organist, blind Dr. J. W. Bischoff, made minor changes, the author added seven verses and a chorus, and the hymn was published shortly afterwards in *Gospel Bells*. Though Dr. Rankin held both D.D. and LL.D. degrees, was for thirteen years president of Washington's Howard University, and wrote scores of hymns, articles, and poems, critics have torn his surviving hymn to shreds. Yet, "God Be With You" is firmly a part of Christian worship around the world and is the one work of its author that has carried his fame through the years.

And so, until we meet again, may God bless you and, in the words of Jeremiah Rankin:

GOD BE WITH YOU

By Jeremiah Rankin, 1828–1904

God be with you till we meet again,
By His counsels guide, uphold you,
With His sheep securely fold you;
God be with you till we meet again.

God be with you till we meet again,
　'Neath His wings protecting hide you,
Daily manna still provide you;
　God be with you till we meet again.

God be with you till we meet again;
　When life's perils thick confound you;
Put His arms unfailing round you;
　God be with you till we meet again.

God be with you till we meet again,
　Keep love's banner floating o'er you,
Smite death's threatening wave before you,
　God be with you till we meet again.

REFRAIN

Till we meet, till we meet,
　Till we meet at Jesus' feet;
Till we meet, till we meet,
　God be with you till we meet again.

Publisher's note: While Mr. Bonner has bid his readers "adieu" with the story of "God Be with You," we are planning a second collection of fifty more stories of "A Hymn Is Born." Volume two of these interesting stories should be off the press as soon as Mr. Bonner can supply us with the material.

THE WILCOX & FOLLETT CO.
Chicago

Index